Praise for The Art of Positive Leadership

"General John Michel embodies an inspiring brand of leadership that values and empowers others, is fiercely focused on building results, and casts a positive and enduring light. With stories gleaned from a lifetime leading courageous and committed warriors on the front line and behind the scenes, Michel illustrates the boundless capabilities of the human spirit."

~**Doug Conant,** Chairman, Avon Products; Chairman, Kellogg Executive Leadership Institute; Founder & CEO, ConantLeadership; Former CEO, Campbell Soup

"General John Michel is a leading light in building a vision, promoting resilience, and serving others. With inspiring stories from the front lines in Afghanistan, and relevant studies from experts, *The Art of Positive Leadership* is a truly worthwhile read."

~**Adam Grant,** Wharton professor and *New York Times* bestselling author of *Give and Take*

"General John Michel is the most highly educated, tech savvy warrior, diplomat & statesman wearing a US military uniform today. His leadership message ranks with the likes of John Maxwell, Tony Robbins, JFK & Martin Luther King, Jr."

~**Geoff De Weaver,** CEO, Touchpoint Entertainment

"As technology and innovation continue to flatten our world, a new generation of leaders is emerging--those who listen and lead from the ground up--rather than from the top down. General John Michel is such a leader, and clearly articulates these changing strategies in *The Art of Positive Leadership*. A must read for any student of life and business!"

~ **Perry Jobe Smith,** Serial Entrepreneur and CEO of Emerson-Byrd, LLC

"Only a handful of leaders have ever led like General John Michel. His ability to develop a team during active combat comprised of multiple countries, languages and cultures resulting in an effective and sustainable Afghan Air Force surpasses most leadership endeavors. His stories will change how you lead and make those around you bette

~ Deb Mills-
University

"In 'The Art of Positive Leadership' John Michel has done a brilliant job of providing a road map for successful leadership at all levels and in all fields whether in business or government. His Sunday Soundbites are an inspiration and invaluable source of guidance to change ourselves and those around us. No matter where you are John has shown that we can make a difference - just as he did in Afghanistan. Why not start today?"

~ **William "Will" M. Fraser, III**, General (Ret), United States Air Force; Senior Executive Leader and Corporate Board Member

"I was honored to have served with General Michel in Afghanistan and observed first hand true leadership in practice under the most difficult conditions - In *The Art of Positive Leadership*, General Michel has captured the essence of the leadership style and skill that made him so successful in a theater of war - he has used a unique blending of axioms and stories, born from the very best leaders, in an amazingly powerful message about the techniques and impact of leaders that unselfishly focus on what can be, what should be, and the people that actually make it happen

~ **John Johns**, Deputy Assistant Secretary of Defense (Maintenance)

"True transformational leadership starts and ends with you. Everyday, you have the opportunity to choose the quality and type of leader you become. Consistently developing the leader within promotes a positive and healthy leader without. General John Michel's book, *The Art of Positive Leadership*, is a must read for leaders looking to pursue a legacy centered around positive transformation."

~ **Mark Cole**, CEO, The John Maxwell Company

"I have known Brig Gen John Michel for nearly 20 years and this book truly sums up his approach to positive leadership! His lessons in *The Art of Positive Leadership*, gleaned from years of frontline service, presents the key elements every leader should know and demonstrate on a daily basis. His ability to teach using experiences from the world of sports, business and even the battlefield brings it all together! I will share this book with all that I meet and mentor!"

~ **CMSgt (Ret) Ken McQuiston**, Former US Transportation Command, Command Senior Enlisted Leader

"A year from now, you could have invested about 20 minutes a week reading General John Michel's newest book, *The Art of Positive Leadership*. With 52 practical, relatable stories at the ready, you'll learn how to encourage people while challenging them to think bigger and build the foundation for a high-performing work environment. At it's core, this book teaches you how to transform everyday, ordinary interactions into opportunities to improve the lives of others. If you want to influence others to greatness, read this book."

~ **Jason W. Womack,** Author of *Your Best Just Got Better*

" What John Michel speaks to in *The Art of Positive Leadership* goes far deeper than the top echelons of his military background. These stories connect to the rich wisdom all leaders need at their disposal. He beautifully communicates how small moments can have huge effects on any organization. From the personal to the epochal, these tenets of leadership serve as a timeless guide for all those on the journey to being a better leader."

~ **Angela Maiers,** Transformative Educator, Author of *The Classroom Habitudes* and Founder of Choose2Matter.org

"In this book, General Michel hits at the heart of what creating High-Performance Teams is all about--empowering others to be a valuable part of the overall mission of the organization! His inspirational work in creating an inclusive environment that encourages everyone to be and do their best resonates deeply in the female sports community. General Michel is way ahead of the curve in his thought process of maximizing individual and collective performance. He is a true visionary in the leadership space!"

~ **Digit Murphy,** Head Coach of the Boston Blades and all-time winningest coach in Division I women's Ice Hockey.

THE ART OF
POSITIVE
LEADERSHIP

BECOMING A PERSON WORTH FOLLOWING

JOHN E. MICHEL

Brigadier General (Ret), USAF
Foreword by David Webb

WESTBOW®
PRESS
A DIVISION OF THOMAS NELSON
& ZONDERVAN

WestBow Press books may be ordered through booksellers or by contacting:

WestBow Press
A Division of Thomas Nelson & Zondervan
1663 Liberty Drive
Bloomington, IN 47403
www.westbowpress.com
1 (866) 928-1240

ISBN: 978-1-4908-6990-2 (sc)
ISBN: 978-1-4908-6991-9 (hc)
ISBN: 978-1-4908-7002-1 (e)

Library of Congress Control Number: 2015902326

Print information is available on the last page.

WestBow Press rev. date: 3/20/2015

To my wife Holly, and my sons, Taylor and
Brandon. Thank you for modeling unconditional
love and selfless service every day;
To my friend and mentor, James (Jim) Bradshaw,
thank you for being such an encouraging
and inspiring others-centered leader;

To those courageous men and women who choose to wear
the clothes of our nation. Thank you for the privilege
of serving alongside you. In honor of your service, it
is my great privilege to donate a portion of the profits
from the sale of this book to the General Leadership
Foundation in support of veteran-related causes.

ACKNOWLEDGMENTS

The Art of Positive Leadership is a labor of love, created amongst some of the most challenging circumstances one could imagine. Written while serving in an active war zone in Afghanistan alongside leaders and warriors from 14 different nations, it draws on experiences and stories accumulated over a quarter-century of military service.

In addition to those men and women in the armed forces who have significantly influenced my own leadership thinking, I would like to offer a special thanks to Robert Greenleaf, John C. Maxwell, Max Lucado, Doug Conant, Ken Blanchard, Mark Miller, James Hunter, Mark Batterson, Mike Myatt, Tim Elmore, Patrick Lencioni, and Peter Marshall.

Most important, I thank Jesus, for providing me with the greatest example of *others-centered* leadership that has ever existed.

CONTENTS

ENCOURAGE

EMPOWER

FOREWORD

What an honor it is to share some thoughts about my good friend John Michel—warrior, leader, servant.

For almost two years I have had the good fortune of observing John's work. Be it shoulder-to-shoulder as a co-host during our monthly one-hour General Leadership forum on SiriusXM Radio, as a featured guest on television, or firsthand in Afghanistan where I had the good fortune of visiting John and his team in Kabul, there is no doubt that when it comes to leadership, John is the real deal.

Having been afforded the rare (if not tumultuous) privilege of being the Department of Defense's go-to positive change agent, he has led three significant and successful multi-billion dollar transformation efforts, the most recent of which includes being given responsibility for leading the 14-nation NATO effort to build a sustainable, independent and capable Afghan Air Force—in an active war zone. The results of his work are nothing short of astounding.

In my many years of working with and for all kinds of leaders, I am proud to say John is in a league of his own. What he and his organization have accomplished in Afghanistan, accelerating development by over three years, saving over $2 billion in taxpayer dollars, and instilling a sense of unprecedented courage and confidence in the Afghan personnel in his care, is unparalleled in both breadth and scope.

What is John's secret to success? He has developed the ability to bring out the very best in those around him, subsequently inspiring those under his command to strive for excellence in support of a cause worth fighting for. John has cracked the code on rejecting mediocrity and pursuing excellence.

In our lives, accepting mediocrity as the norm prevents us from becoming the best possible version of ourselves. Accepting mediocrity keeps us squarely in our comfort zones and subtly persuades us to settle for so much less than we are capable of achieving. For example, despite knowing there is a different way or a different plan that could help us move in the direction of our dreams, aspirations, and objectives, accepting mediocrity convinces us to disengage and simply do or say nothing.

Why shouldn't we? After all, going along with the herd instead of doing something to break from established convention is safe. It can:

Keep us from risking our well thought out career paths;

Prevent us from disrupting our finely honed promotion plans; or

Protect us from venturing too far outside our tightly scripted personal lines of responsibility so we can keep our circumstances secure, predictable, and above all, controllable.

Any way you try to rationalize it, choosing to consistently settle for less than we are capable of doing and being hurts far more than it ever helps.

Please don't get me wrong. We have all undoubtedly found ourselves in that awkwardly comfortable position of settling at one time or another on this journey we call life. The real problem occurs when settling becomes the norm. Like a good habit gone bad, the price of routinely settling for mediocrity and refusing to bring our best selves to whatever it is we are doing can cost us dearly.

The good news is that it doesn't have to remain this way.

As John shares in the pages of this book, all of us, regardless of where we find ourselves in the proverbial hierarchy, social order, or organizational chart, can expand our view of the potential role we can play in the world. How, you ask? Simply by beginning to exert a very powerful form of *positive leadership.*

Increasingly, we find ourselves awash in the flawed ideal that leadership is something reserved for a special few—those amongst us with particular positions, specific titles, or who possess a certain rank or role. Rather than believing we can each use our personal influence to promote a cycle of positive change in our surroundings, we allow ourselves to get stuck in the rut of thinking improving our present circumstances or enhancing current conditions is someone else's responsibility. Fortunately, as you will discover for yourself in *The Art of Positive Leadership*, nothing could be further from the truth. As John reminds us, both by his words and positive example, leadership is making the choice to do the best we can in our present circumstance. It is stepping up and into opportunities to transform the raw material of our lives into something that will add value to the world around us.

Sound too farfetched, or idealistic or straightforward to be true?

Think again.

This collection of 52 Sunday Soundbites from John's time leading a diverse team to previously unthinkable levels of success in Afghanistan serve as bite-sized nuggets of wisdom that will help you elevate your individual and collective performance. They will remind you leadership of yourself and those around you is more verb than simply a noun. It is more about your disposition than position—more about living out the belief that there is no challenge too big to tackle, no solution too elusive to discover when committed to leaving our part of the world better than we found it.

The Art of Positive Leadership: Becoming a Person Worth Following is a must read for everyone who strives to make the most of their personal influence. It serves as a reminder that we each possess immense power to impact the world around us. Use it as a parent, pastor, politician, teacher, soldier, or student. The 52 short stories in this book will equip, encourage, empower and inspire you to remember each and everyone one of us is already as much of a leader as we *choose* to be. Testimony to the reality that leadership, like character, is often revealed in times of crisis, and is developed over the course of anyone's life.

Building an independent, capable and sustainable Air Force in an active war zone is optional.

David Webb
New York City
June 2014

PREFACE

Writing a Better Story

"After nourishment, shelter and companionship,
stories are the thing we need most in the world."
Philip Pullman

I never intended to write this book.

Let me explain.

Nothing fully prepares you to serve in a combat zone. Although it is certainly true that, at the time I was notified I'd been selected to Command the NATO Air Training Command–Afghanistan and 438th Air Expeditionary Wing in Kabul–I had already spent almost a quarter century in uniformed service seemingly preparing for this dynamic assignment. I say dynamic because the mission was to develop an independent, self-sustaining Afghan Air Force ... in an active war zone!

To be clear, it is difficult enough to build an Air Force in peacetime, but being tasked to train and develop sophisticated capabilities and integrate a myriad of technologies while concurrently fighting and winning a war is unprecedented. All, mind you, with limited time, diminishing financial resources, fewer people and scores of logistics and supply challenges. Add in a culture that is hungry for positive change but lacks so many of the elements many of us in western society take for granted and it would be easy to believe we had been asked to pull off mission impossible.

But nothing could be further from the reality of what was actually happening.

You see, despite widespread illiteracy, a resilient and determined enemy, a largely tribal-centered culture, seemingly ever-competing political factions and scores of other factors reflective of a nation that has known nothing but death and devastation for over three decades, progress abounds. Why? One reason—amazing, dedicated, courageous and committed people.

Never in my adult life have I been surrounded by so many inspiring men and women bought in to doing their part towards writing a better story in a nation hungry for hope and change. At no other time in my career did I have the great privilege of working alongside so many accomplished professionals who, despite the daunting nature of their circumstances, choose to selflessly give their best to serve their fellow man. Be it American, Croatian, Greek, French, or any of the fourteen nations under my command, each and every one of those in our organization inspired me daily by their example. And, as their designated leader, I wanted to do something to return the favor.

Having spent decades studying, teaching and applying the tenets of positive-oriented individual and organizational change across the globe, I understand people need to know what they are doing matters. In other words, each of us wants to use our influence to leave our part of the world better than we first found it. We all yearn to be able to do our part to help write a better story.

As human beings, we are moved by stories. Stories stir the soul, engage our hearts, and ignite our imaginations in a way no other medium can. Donald Miller, in his wonderful book, *A Million Miles in a Thousand Years*, shares how humans are alive for the purpose of writing a meaningful story (what he terms a journey), a story played out in essentially three parts.

The first part of our story entails our being born and spending the early years discovering ourselves and the world around us. We then transition into a steady plod through what Miller characterizes as 'a long middle' in which we seek to establish a sense of stability out of natural instability, before ultimately finding ourselves transitioning to an ending that seems designed for reflection. In the final part of our journey, our bodies are slower, the minutes seem to go by faster, and we are prone to work less and celebrate more. All of this leaves us wondering if we have indeed made the most out of the precious, fleeting gift we call life.

What is important to recognize about what Miller is telling us is that our time here on Earth is essentially an epic tale of risk and reward that unfolds before our eyes in real time—the more compelling the narrative, the richer our experience. The key to making the most of our days, then, is not allowing ourselves to get to a point in our journey where we are content settling for "good enough" when we are capable of so much more. Writing a memorable story, one which speaks of leading a life of significance, purpose and meaning, takes work. Great stories never unfold haphazardly. They don't develop by accident. Rather, they are built one day, one experience, one opportunity, and, above all, one relationship at a time.

Which leads me back to the book you are holding in your hand...

As someone who has been blessed to have now led three massive, multi-billion dollar change and transformation efforts and who has been afforded opportunities to lead tens of thousands of people across six continents in both peacetime and wartime, I believe my primary responsibility to those I serve is to equip, encourage, empower and maybe even inspire them to use the raw material of their lives to make the most of their journey. How? By purposefully challenging those around me to continually stretch their thinking and enhance their personal and professional belief in what they are capable of being and doing.

The medium I chose to transform this desire into action in Afghanistan is, not surprisingly, story. Specifically, from my first week on the job in the summer of 2013 I began delivering to all those in my care what I fondly term *The Sunday Soundbite*. I designed these short, 800-1200 word life and leadership essays to stimulate thought, encourage dialogue and, ideally, influence positive action. Each of these brief stories communicates a simple axiom, or practical truth, for the purpose of helping the readers grow into the best possible version of themselves. My hope is that they can do the same for you.

But first, let me tell you the rest of the story.

Within several weeks of my sharing these common sense guidelines for getting the most out of everyday experiences, the *Sunday Soundbite* began taking on a life of its own. Members of our team across Afghanistan began using them to guide professional development conversations on the flight line. Contractors sent me notes asking permission to share them with their employers and fellow employees across the globe. Our English lab teachers even began forwarding them to their students, half a world away. In short order, these simple narratives were consistently emailed home to spouses, sent to executive coaches who began using them with their clients, and have since been featured in a host of periodicals across the planet. And, just like that, the simple act of sharing my personal thoughts on what anyone can do in their personal sphere of influence to try to write a better story rippled across thousands of lives.

Let me pause here so I can put all this in context.

I don't believe for a minute the *Sunday Soundbite* became so popular merely because my storytelling is consistently spectacular. The success of these succinct, practical, portable proverbs goes much deeper. That is, I believe they found such strong resonance because they provide a brief, much-needed respite from life's usual demands and expectations. They helped busy people better understand how they could transform ordinary daily interactions into opportunities to add tangible value into others' lives.

Amidst a daily avalanche of emails, scores of meetings and a steady barrage of requests for our finite time and attention, these short essays helped people momentarily transcend their busyness and invest a couple minutes learning how they could enhance both their personal influence and elevate individual and organizational performance, all for the purpose of maximizing their ability to contribute to writing a better story.

Did this weekly investment make a tangible difference? I'll let you be the judge.

As I mentioned at the outset, our diverse, multinational team faced the prospects of accomplishing something never before attempted in history. Namely, building an independent, sustainable and capable Afghan Air Force comprised of sixty different operational specialties, 119 diverse skills sets, a cradle-to-grave ability to recruit, train, sustain, and retain the human talent needed to successfully employ seven different types of aircraft across their country—simultaneously. Our efforts were further complicated by the fact the decision was made to terminate coalition combat operations several years sooner than anticipated, resulting in significant pressures to reduce costs, accelerate development and consolidate personnel. Despite these added pressures, our organization succeeded in achieving remarkable progress, netting three digit growth in every mission area, accelerating Afghan capability progress by two-and-a-half years, and saving over $2 billion in anticipated costs. In fact, a very senior coalition four-star general deemed our results nothing short of "miraculous."

How did we accomplish this feat? Simple. We emphasized the value of forging positive connections in order to effectively guide and develop others. Yes, we employed a host of well-known processes and approaches to identify efficiencies and refine our methodologies. Yes, we found new, innovative ways to leverage technology to accelerate growth and build confidence. But the key enabler of our superior organizational performance was our highly inclusive, transparent and collaborative means of operating. I believe the genius of our effort was our focus on creating an *others-centered* environment of mutual respect, trust, empowerment, and shared purpose that liberated the latent potential of everyone in our path—American, Brit, Croat, Dane, Greek, Hungarian, El Salvadorian, Ukrainian, Italian, Czech, Canadian, Portuguese, Lithuanian, Mongolian, Latvian, and Afghan, alike.

In simplest terms, we chose to routinely put into practice the attitudes and actions outlined in *The Art of Positive Leadership*.

As I briefly mentioned earlier, axioms are proverbs, or practical truths, designed to teach a valuable (and ideally memorable), life or leadership lesson. Afghans are particularly fond of embedding proverbs within short stories, using them to foster deeper personal connections and bridge diverse backgrounds, cultures, religions, ethnicities, customs, and traditions for the purpose of finding common ground to highlight similarities and celebrate our common humanity.

The book you hold in your hand, filled with 52 short stories represents my humble desire to help those around me improve performance, enhance relationships and elevate personal satisfaction. It speaks to the reality that every day is spring-loaded with possibilities to positively influence how other people think about themselves, their circumstances, and their future. It is my best attempt to share practical ways in which anyone anywhere can help transform a common narrative into an epic story.

Your story. Enjoy.

THE ART OF
POSITIVE
LEADERSHIP

INTRODUCTION

A General's View of Leadership

*"A leader is best when people barely know he
exists, when his work is done, his aim fulfilled,
they will say: we did it ourselves."*
Lao Tzu

The year 1777 was not a particularly good time for America's newly
formed revolutionary army. Under General George Washington's
command, some 11,000 soldiers made their way to Valley Forge.
Following the latest defeat in a string of battles that left Philadelphia
in the hands of British forces, these tired, demoralized, and poorly
equipped early American heroes knew they now faced another
devastating winter.

Yet, history clearly records that, despite the harsh conditions and
lack of equipment that left sentries to stand on their hats to prevent
frostbite to their feet, the men who emerged from this terrible winter
never gave up. Why? Largely because of the inspiring and selfless
example of their leader, George Washington. He didn't ask the members
of his army to do anything he wouldn't do. If they were cold, he was
cold. If they were hungry, he went hungry. If they were uncomfortable,
he, too, chose to experience the same discomfort.

The lesson Washington's profoundly positive example teaches is
that leading people well isn't about driving them, directing them, or

coercing them, it is about compelling them to join you in pushing into new territory. It is motivating them to share your enthusiasm for pursuing a shared ideal, objective, cause, or mission. In essence, it is being *others-centered* instead of self-centered. It is resolving to always conduct yourself in ways that communicate to others that you believe people are always more important than things.

Author Donald Walters provides a powerful example of how this perspective plays out in the most unlikely of places, the battlefield. Walters points out, "The difference between great generals and mediocre ones may be attributed to the zeal great generals have been able to inspire in their men. Some excellent generals have been master strategists, and have won wars on this strength alone. Greatness, however, by very definition implies a great, an expanded view. It transcends intelligence and merely technical competence. It implies an ability to see the lesser in relation to the greater; the immediate in relation to the long term; the need for victory in relations to the needs that will arise once victory has been achieved."

As a general myself, I can confirm that achieving success in my mission, be it in training a new generation of capable men and women for service, promoting peace, or achieving victory in combat, is paramount. Yet, this doesn't imply that I should indiscriminately pursue my goals or blindly pursue my objectives at all costs. What Walters' wise words strive to remind us of is that leadership, be it as a general in the military, an executive in the boardroom, a pastor serving a congregation, or a parent providing for a family, isn't about exercising power over people, rather, it's about finding effective ways to work with people so they can grow into the leaders they are capable of becoming.

*   *   *

In 400 B.C., Xenophon, a skilled military leader and pupil of Socrates, was the first to record a definition of leadership in the western world. In his work, *Oeconomicus*, Xenophon writes "It is highly indicative of good leadership when people obey someone without coercion and are prepared to remain by him during time of danger." This perspective, as it turns out, was grounded in his strong belief that the primary role of a leader (whom he referred to as a general) was to take care of the community while respecting the freedom and dignity of the individuals who comprise that community.

Doug Conant, former CEO of Campbell Soup and current Chairman of Avon once reminded me, leadership isn't easy. The pressure to constantly meet deadlines, consistently achieve or exceed performance targets, and effectively mobilize others towards a common goal or objective are ever-present realities of the world in which we must operate. Nonetheless, I am convinced the reason Doug continues to experience eye-watering success wherever he serves, stems from his belief that successful leadership isn't about *him*—it's about creating conditions for *others* around him to flourish and thrive and come fully alive.

Doug, much like Xenophon centuries before him, understands the best leaders are approachable, relatable, and aspirational. They are positive, *others-centered* doers who strive to build things, grow things, and move things steadily forward by intentionally investing the best of themselves in those who comprise their team, tribe, community, or family. As he eloquently points out in his book, *Touchpoints*, leaders "... shape the future by doing something better or bolder or more exciting. Unlike many who only dream of creating a better future, leaders are the dreamers who get things done, and the way they do it is by (positively) influencing others."

*   *   *

Those who serve under an effective general, CEO, school superintendent, politician or parent, know well that he or she must be both tough and tender, appropriately balancing love and discipline; grace and accountability; hope and reality. They understand he or she would ask nothing of others that they would not first do themselves. Such a leader believes with all their heart that they are one with their people, not superior to them. They know that they are simply doing a job together.

I am convinced that now is the time to remember the most effective form of leadership is positive. It is collaborative. It is never assigning a task, role, or function to another that we ourselves would not be willing to perform.

Now is the time to accept that leadership is meant to be more verb than noun, more active than passive. More about being others-centered than self-centered.

Now is the time to not lose sight of the fact that people, be it in warfare, politics, religion, education, or business, are always more important than things. Are you game?

THE POSITIVE
LEADERSHIP MODEL

*"If we take care of the moments, the
years will take care of themselves."*
Maria Edgeworth

Serge LeClerc became the co-leader of one of the largest drug crime families in Canada at a very young age. Although no one knows just how many lives he diminished or destroyed, today, he's working to be a positive influence to the very addicts who once were his clients.

Here's his story.

LeClerc was born in an abandoned building in eastern Canada, a product of rape, to a single, 13-year-old girl who had run away from home. Together, teen mom and baby eventually moved into the inner city of Toronto, where young Serge literally brought himself up.

At the age of eight, he began skipping school and ended up being admitted to a residential training facility, where he was abused. Like his mom, he, too, became a runaway. Living in abandoned buildings and garages, he routinely ate out of garbage cans.

By age 15, a desperate and disenfranchised LeClerc found himself a member of one of the largest, toughest street gangs in Toronto. As a teenager, he routinely carried a gun, ran alcohol stills, and directed extortion rackets. In 1967, he became one of Canada's largest drug dealers. For 20 years, he was addicted to his own product, while steadily rising in the power hierarchy of Canada's criminal underworld.

In 1984, he was arrested in a $40 million drug bust and began a nine-year term.

One day in prison, he encountered a volunteer who told him he had a choice. He could choose to believe he was someone who had no particular purpose and continue to live to please only himself. Or, he could accept he was someone of unique value who possessed the power to add significant, positive value to others lives.

LeClerc was not easily convinced, so he shrugged off the volunteer's words.

Seven months later, however, after watching a 19-year-old man commit suicide in the next cell, a man who had gotten himself in that position from using Serge's own lab and drug dealer network, he remembered the volunteer's words. And on a quiet morning in 1985, LeClerc, one of the most violent men in the Canadian penitentiary system, changed his heart and committed to using the remainder of his days to selflessly serve those around him.

When he was finally released in 1988, he founded the first chapter of *Prison Fellowship in Canada*, and today, works with *Teen Challenge* in Saskatchewan as a regional director. And in perhaps the most intriguing twist of all, he has been asked to serve those around him as a Member of the Saskatchewan Legislature. The once ruthless lawbreaker, now a committed lawmaker, is making good on his commitment to transform life's millions of ordinary moments into opportunities to be more others-centered rather than self-centered.

* * *

As the story of Serge LeClerc so powerfully illustrates, the truest measure of leadership success stems from our willingness to become *others-centered.*

Being others-centered means our energy and attention is positively directed toward those around us. It is recognizing that achieving true happiness in life isn't just about fulfilling your own agenda or pursuing your own personal ambition. It is, above all else, using your influence to enrich people's lives by selflessly serving others, unconditionally loving others, and generously striving to build lasting value into others...one conversation, engagement, and opportunity at a time.

The excessive infatuation with individualism that has washed over so much of our society the past 30 years has made service to others an elusive goal. As business leader Mark Lukens so astutely shares, "These decades of rampant self-indulgence tried to teach us that business and leadership were all about looking after number one, and that everything else would follow from that."

Yet nothing could be further from the truth.

The warning signs that our society is experiencing a very real *personal leadership* crisis are everywhere. You only need to turn on the TV, tune into a radio program, click on the Internet, or pick up any periodical to find that story after story recounts a sad, sordid tale of broken promises, plundered pensions, and selfish motives by many of those entrusted to positions of authority and responsibility. In once high-flying companies such as Lehman Brothers, Enron, Arthur Anderson, WorldCom, and Tyco, it was the leaders' apathy, inaction, or lack of accountability that directly led to millions of innocent people being negatively impacted, forever.

Of course, lapses in leadership are not limited to just the business world. For example, the seemingly endless string of politicians, pastors, teachers, and soldiers, facing ethical and moral indiscretions continue to shake our confidence in leaders at every level. Perhaps it should be no surprise then that almost 80 percent of respondents in a recent Gallup poll think the moral values of our nation are getting worse instead of better. And according to a survey conducted by Harvard University, a majority of Americans believe we suffer from a serious leadership crisis in America. Perhaps more importantly, even more believe the United States will decline as a nation without better leaders.

Fortunately, we each possess within ourselves the ability to help turn this trend around.

See the Leader, Know the Followers

Before we continue, let me take a moment to ask you a couple of important questions:

- Do you believe leaders at any and every level can use themselves as a catalyst for positive change?
- Is it possible to conduct ourselves in a more optimistic, courageous and compelling manner in order to infuse our surroundings with a greater sense of possibility and life-giving positivity?
- How would things improve in our homes, workplaces, worship spaces, and communities if leaders balanced their need for vision casting, planning, strategy, and execution with a tangible commitment to engaging the imaginations and inspiring the actions of those they lead?
- What could happen in your own life if you were more intentional in how you thought, felt, talked, and acted towards others?

Though the answers to these questions may vary from reader to reader, what is certain is this: living up and into your greatest leadership potential depends largely on your willingness to maximize the investment of time, talent, and energy into the lives of those around you.

Positive, others-centered leaders understand this. They innately believe everyone desires to grow into the fullness of their potential. They recognize their primary responsibility (and opportunity) as leaders is to use their influence to try to leave their part of the world better than they first found it. Not by developing more followers, mind you, but by willfully growing more leaders.

Just as any sports coach dreams of a team full of superstars, organizations strive for the same. Be it a school, business office, fast food restaurant, church, or political campaign, it is reasonable to assert the greater the available talent, the greater the potential to achieve extraordinary results. But developing a deep bench of confident, capable, and committed *others-centered* leaders doesn't happen by accident. It takes a deliberate and proactive effort to transform good people into great leaders.

With this in mind, what I discovered in my over quarter century journey of studying, observing and ultimately, putting into practice the attitudes and actions of the world's most effective positive change leaders, is that all of them focus their energy and attention in four primary areas. Specifically, they make the most of every opportunity to be others-centered by willfully *equipping, encouraging, empowering,* and *inspiring* those around them to raise the bar on their own leadership potential, themselves. Here's how.

> **Equip** – The positive leader recognizes that the most effective way to engage others in reframing how they think and feel about their potential is to equip each member of the team with new opportunities to learn and grow. This learning is more 'learn by doing', whereby the leader motivates others to apply their unique strengths, gifts, talents and skills in order to develop a more constructive, optimistic view of their circumstances. In equipping people to discover what interests them, the positive leader ignites a sense of passion and possibility within others that transforms routine interactions into opportunities to build relationships of mutual trust, respect, and understanding.

> **Encourage** – The positive leader believes that a critical responsibility of leaders is to synthesize diverse views into a compelling vision. As a result, they encourage new ideas from those around them, motivating people toward higher levels of achievement by enhancing others' sense of belonging. At the same time, they create an environment for those around them to adopt a broader perspective, accept a sense of hope and possibility that motivates them to move out in new directions, and encourages them to take smart risks in pursuit of a compelling purpose.

Empower – The positive leader makes it a priority to coach and mentor those around them, facilitating improvement, enhancing ownership, and promoting wide-spread empowerment. Rather than relying on coercing, demanding, or directing others to act, they prefer to bypass traditional forms of command-and-control leadership in favor of generously sharing power with those around them. By broadly trusting others to think and act for themselves, positive leaders affirm their belief that rewarding people for their courage, tenacity, and resilience, is one of the most powerful ways to help others overcome their fears and embrace the growth that comes from prudently challenging the status-quo.

Inspire — The positive leader understands the most powerful form of power and influence we wield originates within us—manifesting as the attitudes and actions we choose to routinely model to those around us. Understanding the magic of role modeling is that it works at any age, in any place, and at any time; positive leaders choose to *inspire* others by their example. As leadership expert John Maxwell likes to say, "The more you walk, the less you have to talk. Live the life in front of the ones you seek to influence."

It's a long standing truth that people reflect their leaders. Study after study confirms how well a leader wields their influence in creating an environment for those around them to flourish and thrive and come fully alive is the single most important factor in determining individual contribution and collective performance. In the words of Albert Schweitzer, "Example is not the main thing in influencing others . . . it is the only thing." People emulate what they see modeled. Positive model, positive response. Negative model, negative response. What leaders do, the potential leaders around them do. What they prioritize and value, their people prioritize and value. Leaders set the tone.

Positive Leadership is Choosing to be Others-Centered …One Interaction at a Time

One late spring morning, in a third-grade classroom in a quiet, Midwestern town, a nine-year-old boy named Danny sits quietly at his desk. All of a sudden, a small puddle begins to appear between his feet. He struggles to imagine how this has happened as he tries to hide the fact that his pants are wet. After all, it's never happened before, and he knows that when the other boys in the class find out what happened, he will never hear the end of it. Or worse, when the girls find out, they'll never speak to him again as long as he lives.

Danny is convinced this is the end of the world as he knows it.

Just about then, he sees his teacher approaching with a look in her eyes that says he's been found out. She is onto his embarrassing, shameful secret!

As the teacher is walking toward him, a classmate named Susie is carrying a goldfish bowl that is filled with water. Susie trips in front of the teacher and inexplicably dumps the bowl of water in Danny's lap.

Now, all of a sudden, instead of being the object of ridicule, Danny is the object of people's empathy and attention. The teacher rushes him downstairs and gives him a pair of gym shorts to put on while his pants dry out. The other children in the class are on their hands and knees cleaning up around his desk. And in the blink of an eye, the ridicule that should have been his has been transferred to someone else—Susie. Although Susie tries to help clean up the mess she created, the other children tell her to go away. After all, to them, she is a klutz who has already done enough damage for one day.

Finally, at the end of the day, as they are both waiting for the bus, Danny walks over to Susie and whispers, "You did that on purpose, didn't you?"

Susie whispers back, "I wet my pants once, too."

Parting Thoughts

All of us have likely experienced a Danny kind of moment. That is, we've done something that we instantly regret or suddenly find ourselves in a situation where we are embarrassed, ashamed, or afraid.

For some, the memories of these events still causes us to wince. The absence of empathy, compassion, and caring by an insensitive supervisor, coach, or coworker in those moments of our greatest vulnerability has left a lasting, negative impression that is difficult to shake.

On the other hand, the odds are high you've also experienced a Susie-type response, being the beneficiary of unexpected grace and kindness by a sensitive teacher, kind counselor, close friend, or empathetic parent.

Psychiatrist Alfred Adler described this powerful ability to reach beyond ourselves and selflessly support another as the willingness "to see with the eyes of another, to hear with the ears of another, and to feel with the heart of another." I like to think of this people-centered commitment as *otherliness,* or the desire to connect to those around us in a heartfelt, meaningful way.

Admittedly, to some people, a term like otherliness is viewed as soft or touchy-feely. It may be appropriate in the classroom but it has no place in the boardroom. Despite what some mistakenly think, practicing otherliness is not some sort of "I'm okay, you're okay" mushiness. As a leader, it doesn't mean we insist on making other people's feelings our own or trying to be liked, loved, or even approved by others. If we did that, we would rarely get anything done! Instead, otherliness is intentionally making what is important to others important to us. It is being aware of other people's feelings, making a point to value the viewpoints of those around you, and being open to creating a space or environment where people feel safe to attempt growing into the best possible version of themselves.

In this vein, scientists studying human nature are reporting that our society is undergoing a revolutionary shift in how we understand how people, organizations, and entire cultures flourish, thrive, and come fully alive. Specifically, they confirm how our brains are wired at birth for social cooperation and mutual aid. Hence, if the 20th century was the age of introspection, when self-help and therapy culture encouraged us to believe that the best way to understand who we are and how to live was to look inside ourselves, the 21st century should become *the age of otherliness*, where we discover true success and satisfaction can only be achieved by becoming genuinely interested and invested in the lives of others. I am convinced that otherliness should be the impetus for a new revolution. I'm not talking an old-fashioned revolution built on stringent laws, stoic institutions, or stifling policies, but a radical revolution in leadership and human relationships that enables us to:

Equip others to experience less frustration and more consideration;

Encourage others to promote less separation and more unification;

Empower others to strive for less dissatisfaction and more appreciation; and

Inspire others to fear less, love more, and do their part to leave their part of the world better than they first found it.

Consider otherliness a transformation that manifests the Susie or Serge LeClerc in all of us. It is a learned art motivated by a selfless heart. It is a means of, in the words of author Leo Buscaglia, "to quit underestimating the power of a touch, a smile, a kind word, a listening ear, an honest compliment, or the smallest act of caring" to transform even the most difficult, discouraging, or distressing moment into an opportunity to live out our belief we are at our best when we are operating in service to those around us...

...one Danny at a time.

HOW TO GET THE MOST
FROM THIS BOOK

Each day, we make dozens of decisions that influence the trust people have in our leadership and the commitment they have to the organization. That is why it is so important we consistently show up in a manner that communicates our effectiveness, competence, and heartfelt interest in those around us. As leader's intent to leave our part of the world better than we first found it, we must connect meaningfully. In every interaction.

Demonstrating we are someone worth following demands we bring more than our agenda and mere information to our interactions. We have to bring our very best selves. As Doug Conant reminds us, "Today's employees are savvy and avid consumers of media and communications. They can smell spin and disingenuousness a mile away. Before they choose to engage fully, they want (and deserve) more than just a company face and corporate platitudes. They want to know they are dealing with a real person who says what they mean – and does what they say they will do."

Sociologists and neuroscientists assert that every person has a number of fundamental needs that must be met in order to grow into the best possible version of themselves. These include:

- To be valued and appreciated;
- To feel secure;
- To be treated fairly;
- To be accepted;

- To learn and achieve;
- To exercise responsibility and autonomy;
- To experience a sense of belonging;
- To contribute to something purposeful and meaningful.

Though this list is certainly not all-inclusive, it does reflect those elements a leader can intentionally influence in their surroundings each and every day. At a time in history when we need to reduce people's fear of failure, enhance their sense of responsibility, and increase their personal and professional ability to grow into their full potential, we need an ethical and moral approach to leadership that imparts a deep sense of confidence within others. We need others-centered leaders who are willing to *equip, encourage, empower,* and *inspire* those around them to become the leaders they are capable of becoming.

And this book can help you do just that.

I arranged the following *Sunday Soundbites* into four sections corresponding to the four dimensions of Positive Leadership (Equip, Encourage, Empower, and Inspire). My goal in doing so is to provide you with a simple, practical framework you can use to practice being others-centered in your interactions. At the same time, as a leader I know how challenging it can be to constantly seek new ideas, stories, and concepts to promote high performance in your sphere of influence. This is why I hope you will use this book as a practical resource. After all, the goal is simple:

Equip you with tools to improve your leadership effectiveness;

Encourage you to modify or adjust anything and everything you find of value for the purpose of enhancing your effectiveness;

Empower you to try new ways of thinking and being and;

Inspire you to be others-centered in all dimensions of your life.

A couple of final thoughts before you get started:

Believe this book is written for you. I wrote these stories to be used by you in your own unique environment. I hope you will choose to share them where and when they add value to your own leadership journey.

Read this book with a goal in mind. Read this book believing there is at least one idea, concept, or discovery that can enhance your own leadership effectiveness. Stay alert to what resonates most.

Take Notes as you read. Write notes *to yourself* in the margins, at the beginning and end of chapters, or on any of the blank pages in the book. If you are reading his book in digital format, then keep a small notepad handy to capture your thoughts and ideas.

Finally, resolve to practice what you preach. The more you strive to hold yourself accountable to your commitment to be a positive, *others-centered* leader, the better you will do. Resolve to improve a little bit every day. If you fall short, get back up, and do your best to improve next time. If you consistently 'walk the talk', others will believe your promise, and will fight their hardest to do better too, right alongside you.

Admittedly, there are no one-size-fits-all solutions to the host of challenges we face as leaders. Choosing to practice an *others-centered* approach to leading, however, is certainly a significant step in the right direction. By focusing on developing a well of physical, intellectual, emotional, and spiritual strength in those we encounter in our sphere of influence, we create the conditions to transform good people into great leaders.

As you prepare to explore the words I penned for my multinational team while deployed to Afghanistan, please remember, the concepts, perspectives and practices presented in these 52 short stories are intended to paint familiar pictures illustrating unfamiliar truths. They are designed to make you a more effective leader by helping you communicate in word and deed you are someone worth following.

The Art of Positive Leadership will prepare you to more effectively achieve goals within your environment. It is a book about elevating your own leadership ability—first by the way you lead your own life, then by the way you lead others.

PARTING THOUGHTS: Leadership combines both heart and art. To possess one without the other is to fall short of achieving ones full, positive potential. Hence, in simplest terms, *others-centered* leadership is about adding value, not accumulating perks. It's about choosing to use your influence to willingly, even enthusiastically, make the development of those in our care your foremost priority.

With this in mind, I am excited to share I've developed an easy to use companion website to capture examples of leaders putting into practice the *others-centered* leadership principles outlined in this book. At www.JohnEMichel.com, you can upload short videos or share stories of those around you who are making the development of others a tangible priority. My hope is, by offering a simple means of capturing real-world stories of people operating at their best, *otherliness* will affirm that which gives our life the greatest meaning, purpose, and direction, comes from routinely promoting service over self-interest.

In the words of Facebook Chief Operating Officer and *Lean In* author Sheryl Sandberg, "Leadership is about making others better as a result of your presence and making sure that impact lasts in your absence." My hope is you will take what you will find in the following pages to heart and resolve to be the positive leader you want to be and others deserve to see.

Beginning right where you are today.

EQUIP

Others-centered leaders provide those around them the best chance at success in any given task, assignment, or circumstance. They refuse to merely delegate and disappear, choosing instead to equip others with the tools required to become the leader they can be and others deserve to see.

1

Create a Strategy for Sustainable Success

"A goal without a plan is just a wish."
Antoine de Saint-Exupéry

Growing up, one of my favorite television series was *Mission: Impossible*. The immensely popular program chronicles the adventures of the Impossible Missions Force (IMF), a team of government spies and specialists who are regularly offered "impossible missions" (should they decide to accept them).

Outside of the cool gadgets and spectacular stunts, what I most enjoyed about the series was that it reinforced how, with a well-executed, methodical strategy, just about anything's possible. Take a lesson from a real life mission impossible, the race to be the first to the South Pole, as a case-in-point.

In 1911, a steady, thoughtful, and somewhat reserved Roald Amundsen headed up the Norwegian team in the great race to be first to stake a claim to walking on the South Pole. At the exact same time, flamboyant adventurist, Robert Scott, directed a team from England intent on achieving the same objective. The two expeditions faced exactly the same unforgiving weather conditions, terrain, and obstacles. They both possessed exactly the same technology, the most sophisticated of its day. All their equipment was virtually identical.

Yet, Amundsen and his team reached the South Pole thirty-four days ahead of Scott.

So what made the difference?

A well-executed, methodical plan. You see, Amundsen was a tireless and talented strategist. He understood that achieving extraordinary goals demands setting conditions for success before you begin. In other words, he innately understood that making the seemingly impossible, possible demands you consistently follow a deliberate series of steps that will set the conditions for your success.

For Amundsen and his team, this translated into breaking down their ambitious endeavor into a series of (literally) daily objectives. Specifically, he and his team had to cover fifteen to twenty miles a day. No more, no less. In bad weather (and there is plenty at the South Pole from what I understand), they traveled fifteen to twenty miles. In good weather? You guessed it, fifteen to twenty miles.

Steady. Consistent. Committed.

Scott, on the other hand, was irregular in his approach and outright erratic in execution. Instead of adopting a deliberate, measurable methodology, his team opted to push to exhaustion when the weather was good and decided to stay put when the weather was bad. Two leaders, both with the exact same impossible sized dream, with drastically different approaches. And, perhaps not surprisingly, both achieved two very dramatically different outcomes.

Amundsen and his team won the race without losing a single man. They were the first to achieve something people, for generations, had deemed impossible. Conversely, Scott lost not only the race but lost his life and lives of every person he was leading. For them, the mission proved not only impossible, but, sadly, fatal. All for lack of a well-executed, methodical strategy for success.

*   *   *

In the military, we take strategy seriously. Strategy enables an individual, team, or organization to know where they are, where they are going, and informs the path to take to reach their desired destination. Developing a smart strategy translates intention into focused action. It transforms bold goals into inspiring realities.

As you set out to pursue your dreams and desires, I'd like to encourage you to consider tackling an ambitious "Mission: Impossible" size goal of your own. Whether it's a personal goal, such as adopting a healthier lifestyle, an organizational goal such as being a more effective supervisor, or a societal goal such as doing something to end childhood hunger in your city, here are proven insights from my last two plus decades of creating strategies for sustainable success you can leverage to propel yourself and those you lead into new challenging, yet immensely rewarding, territory.

Plan on Making Mistakes: Fear of falling short keeps many people living small. Don't buy the lie that failure is fatal. Life is not about finding yourself, it is about creating yourself...one opportunity at a time. You have to take chances to make your dreams a reality. Don't be afraid of making mistakes. In fact, plan to make lots of them! Your odds for success will increase with the number of deliberate decisions you make and active steps you take in the direction of your goals.

Learn How to Say No: In our hurried society, being busy is celebrated. Saying yes to doing more seems to be the path of the high achiever. Don't buy that lie. The truth is, not everything is worth doing. Although saying yes supports risk-taking, embodies courage, and reflects a willingness to lead an open-hearted life of seemingly inexhaustible opportunity, knowing when to say no is what will actually keep you on track. Remember, you are the agent of your own limits. Commit to saying no if it will keep you moving forward in the direction of your deepest goals, dreams, and desires.

Always Make Deliberate Choices: The decisions you make every day can change your life forever. You do not choose to be born. You do not choose your parents. You do not choose the country of your birth. You do not choose the circumstances of your upbringing. Despite this whole realm of choicelessness, you can, and do, choose how you will live. So live to be intentionally productive. Quit tracking your time and start tracking your results. Put first things first and resolve to get the right things done. Avoid low-value added distractions. Choose to stay true to those things in your plan.

Never Underestimate Your Personal Power: I'm sure there were many times in the quest for the South Pole that Roald Amundsen and his crew felt they couldn't go on. I'm confident they encountered numerous moments when they felt the goal was too bold, the dream too big, and the next step too difficult. Nonetheless, history confirms they did not allow the momentary challenges to paralyze them, the present difficulty to overwhelm them, or the fear of failure to intimidate them. Imagine what you could accomplish if you too believed no dream was too big, no challenge too daunting, and no mission was impossible.

Although I cannot be there to see you step up to a life lived with intensity, purpose, and meaning as you grow into your full leadership potential, know my best wishes go with you. I encourage you to cherish every second, every moment. Seize them all – to accomplish, to celebrate, to act, to be your best self. Do not imitate anyone else. Have patience with your dreams and be deliberate in executing your plan. Live as if this is your last day.

Be Steady. Consistent. Committed. Believe achieving your mission is absolutely possible.

2

Be Grace-Full

"I do not at all understand the mystery of
grace - only that it meets us where we are but
does not leave us where it found us."
Anne Lamott

A popular Russian tale recounts how when Nicholas II was the Czar of Russia, a father enlisted his son in the military with the hope of instilling discipline and direction in his life. Among other things, the young man had a weakness for gambling, and the conditions of military life seemed to hurt rather than help.

His army job was bookkeeping. As his gambling debts grew, he borrowed money from the outpost treasury to pay his debts. He kept losing instead of winning and sank deeper and deeper into debt.

One night, contemplating his horrible situation, he added up his debts. When he saw the immense total, he wrote across the ledger, "So great a debt, who can pay?" He decided to take his own life. He sat back in his chair, gun in hand, to reflect for a few minutes. As he contemplated the sad conditions of his life and his impending death, he dozed off.

Czar Nicholas II was inspecting the outpost that night. When he entered the bookkeeper's shack, he saw the sleeping man, the loaded gun, and the revealing ledger.

When the soldier awoke, he stared at the ledger in disbelief, reading the words, "So great a debt, who can pay?" Underneath were the words, "Paid in full, Czar Nicholas II!"

Can you imagine how this young man must have felt in that moment? After all, given his countless mistakes and racking up debt he could never possibly repay, here he was with balanced books—a clean slate. Despite doing nothing to warrant such generosity, he was now a free man. His new chance at life was an unwarranted and unexpected gift from the most unlikely of sources.

*   *   *

The Greek's have a term that beautifully captures the essence of this illustration. It is the verb *charis*, from which we derive the term grace. To the Greeks, anything of beauty, favor, or delight in which a person could rejoice was a form of *grace*. In our contemporary translation, grace enjoys an even deeper, more profound translation, meaning the willful exercise of love, kindness, mercy, favor; or disposition to benefit or serve another. In essence, grace is a word synonymous with showing unmerited concern or favor to someone. And, as the example of Czar Nicholas II affirms, it's not necessarily because someone deserves it, but simply because we choose to freely grant it.

Admittedly, extending grace is not always easy. In our own lives, it means intentionally loving the unlovable, those who seem intent on stretching rules, pushing our buttons, even talking poorly of us, and to us. Extending grace also means we choose to respond contrary to our natural inclinations. For instance, instead of responding with a glare, a sharp retort, or with icy silence when someone has frustrated, insulted, or wrongly accused us, we choose instead to treat the other person better than they have chosen to treat us.

Does extending grace as a leader really matter, you may wonder? Without a doubt! Authors Bill Thrall, Bruce McNicol, and Ken McElrath in their book, *The Ascent of a Leader*, share how environments where grace abounds are characterized by higher satisfaction, increased engagement, improved trust, and heightened productivity. They add how leaders who are grace-full help people feel safe to be themselves, to live authentically, celebrate each other, laugh more frequently, and extend grace themselves more liberally. In an organization where grace abounds, it's common to find a supportive atmosphere, where the seeds of mutually satisfying relationships are frequently and intentionally planted and nurtured and people do not feel constrained by strict adherence to a particular set of do's and don'ts to feel accepted, affirmed, or appreciated. Given these profoundly positive effects, what can you do today to begin being more Grace-*Full* in your own sphere of influence? Start by:

- Intentionally speaking words that build up, not tear down;
- Focusing more on others needs rather than merely satisfying your own;
- Saying, "I'm sorry" and "I was wrong" without being afraid;
- Not always keeping score of what is fair;
- Not condemning or giving up on people; and
- Taking every opportunity to emphasize mercy, not justice.

Extending grace is how others-centered leaders respond to mistakes and errors. It reflects a mature understanding that others rarely (if ever) fail or fall short of our expectations because they intend to. Grace, then, is the universal currency of mutually-respectful and beneficial relationships. It is being present for another, believing the best in another, and striving to enhance the well-being of another.

The fact of the matter is, if you want to create a high-performing organization, then you have to be willing to extend grace. I'm not saying you have to dismiss poor performance, overlook situations you know are wrong, or not hold people accountable for failing to achieve established standards. But I am telling you that unless grace is present, people will not take risks, they won't learn and grow in their own leadership abilities, and they will fear failure so much, they won't even get close to achieving their individual potential—making it difficult to impossible for the organization to reach its potential as well.

So the next time you find it difficult to extend unmerited concern or favor to someone when they fail, fall short of your expectations, or just plain frustrate you to no end, remember the lesson of Czar Nicholas II: Grace is one of the most important gifts a leader can offer their people. Grace, the willful exercise of love, kindness, mercy, favor; or disposition to benefit or serve another, is as much a treasure we bestow on others as it is a treasure we share with ourselves.

Whose ledger can you balance today? Whose slate can you wipe clean so they can begin anew?

3

Bend But Don't Break

"A good half of the art of living is resilience."
Alain de Botton

More than two million people died, four million were displaced and thousands fled civil war. However, through faith and perseverance, one "lost boy," who later grew to become an American Airman, returned home healthier and happier than ever before.

Airmen Magazine recently featured the story of Air Force Staff Sergeant Deng Pour who, as a young boy at the age of 5, lived through many years of near starvation and genocide resulting from the 1983-2006 Sudanese civil war. Amazingly, he never gave up.

Sergeant Pour's early life in Sudan was filled with gunfire, violence and moving from village to village to survive. One night, Sudanese government troops ambushed a nearby township, forcing Pour and dozens of other refugees to escape across the border to Ethiopia. Though there was very little to eat, they were safe. Eventually, he made his way to a refugee camp in northern Kenya where he, and thousands of other southern Sudanese children, became known as the "lost boys of Sudan."

At the camp, Pour attended school and learned basic reading, writing and arithmetic. For the next five years, life gradually improved. In time, Pour was given the opportunity to travel to the United States.

After receiving his green card and graduating from high school, he chose to join the Air Force as a Chaplain's assistant.

Pour has served in the military for seven years and is currently back in Africa as the Non-Commissioned Officer in charge of religious affairs for the Combined Joint Task Force-Horn of Africa. In this capacity, he works in a variety of support roles building morale among the combined forces, and assists other partner nations' militaries with improving their military chaplaincies.

"My goal in Africa is simple: to make a difference, whether it's amongst my peers or in this country," Pour said. *"As I was going through my struggles, many people went out of their way to help me ... The Air Force is a way for me to give back, to serve my adopted country because I know I'm representing something greater than myself."*

And what a difference he is making. His positive leadership serves as a tangible symbol of resilience of mind, body and soul to countless people everywhere. He is an others-centered leader who teaches that life circumstances will certainly bend us but they don't necessarily have to break us.

*   *   *

Once in a great while, we learn of an organization or a person who has performed so much better than expectations, it is difficult to believe this level of success is possible. You've heard the narrative: Someone like Staff Sgt. Deng Pour who, by all reasonable measures has the odds stacked against them, somehow manages to transcend their situation and achieve remarkable success. They are the person we long to emulate, who manages to transform difficulties into positive life-changing realities. The person who finds a way to tap into a reservoir of resilience that leaves us scratching our heads and wondering, "How can I do the same?"

Resilience is not a new term in academic, healthcare, business, or military circles. In fact, the view that resilience is central to consistently operating at high performance has been gaining attention among researchers over the last 25 years. At the same time, studies have increasingly shown that the way people choose to show-up in the world, despite the challenges they face in any given moment, is at the heart of being an effective leader.

Unfortunately, many of us still mistakenly believe this thing we call resilience is some elusive "some have it, some don't" type of quality. Yet nothing could be further from the truth. Resilience is available to each of us. It's an attitude that informs our actions. It's a way of thinking and being that equips us to turn loss into gain; to transform tragedy into triumph; to operate at peak positive performance in good times and tough times.

I know because I personally discovered the value of possessing resilience, or the hardship that ensues in its absence, years ago.

A Devastating Day

I'll never forget that summer day in 2000. I was trotting away on the treadmill at the base gym in California when my wife walked in and said we needed to talk. Admittedly, to a husband, these words alone are cause for alarm. Did I leave the tub running when I left the house and flooded the living room? Did I miss a key appointment, anniversary or other important event? Did I fail to adequately close the door to our children's hamster colony and now our house was awash in scurrying rodent's intent to wreak havoc at will?

I didn't know the topic but I could tell from her tone and expression, something was very amiss. So I hit the stop button and followed her into the hallway. Her next words literally took my breath away: "There is no easy way to tell you this, but Kyle is dead. He took his own life yesterday afternoon."

Now let me put this in context for you. Kyle and I were college roommates and longtime friends. Kyle and I enjoyed Texas-size adventures together; our families had periodically vacationed together; and I considered him one of my most trusted confidants. To hear he was suddenly dead was disturbing. Hearing he had taken his own life was devastating.

I jumped in my car and immediately called Kyle's wife. In the midst of what was one of the toughest phone calls in my life, I passed my deepest sympathy and checked in on their two small children. Both were under six years old. It was clear she was still in shock. So I did what my heart told me was right and boarded a plane that afternoon for San Antonio, Texas. I stayed two weeks and helped the stunned, grieving family work through this challenging period. To this day, I miss Kyle's precious friendship but am grateful knowing his family has gone on to rebuild their lives.

The life lesson I took away from this personal period of heartache is that equipping ourselves to endure challenging circumstances and tough seasons is an ongoing endeavor. Developing personal resilience, the external manifestation, of the internal belief that we can endure life's setbacks, is what allows us to make healthy choices when our burdens threaten to overload us and our present circumstances begin to overwhelm us.

If anyone would have asked me, Kyle would have been the last person I would have expected to take his own life. He had a beautiful family, was materially wealthy and was essentially a GQ poster-model. In fact, I witnessed him literally stop traffic on more than one occasion simply by flashing that famous, white-toothed perfect smile. He also possessed a Texas-sized heart, generously sharing all he had with those around him. But his tragic loss demonstrates how the external can so easily mask a terribly tormented interior. Despair, discouragement, fear, mental illness, and a host of other invisible enemies can wreak havoc with our heads, our hearts and ultimately, our lives.

I share this very personal story with you because the difference in outcomes between Staff Sgt. Deng Pour and my late friend Kyle is *Resilience*. Pour developed the coping skills to confront personal crisis and effectively deal with hardship. He was unafraid to reach out for help, to lean on others, and to consistently improve his ability to deal with life's setbacks. Sadly, Kyle didn't.

Over the last 14 years, I have become somewhat of a zealot for developing personal resilience. I've made it a priority to fortify my psyche so I can be adequately prepared to ride the waves of adversity rather than being pulled under by the torrent wrought by adversity. I have chosen to enhance my ability to prepare for emotional emergencies and become more adept at accepting what comes at me with flexibility rather than responding with rigidity. In simplest terms, I've adopted and internalized the old metaphor that resilient people are like bamboo in a hurricane--they bend rather than break. And although I may feel at times as though I'm momentarily broken, there is always a part of me deep inside that knows I won't stay that way forever. This is the essence of resilience and I'm convinced it is a must-have commodity in today's leadership environment.

Before wrapping up this chapter, let me leave you with several practical considerations on how you too can strengthen your personal resilience:

- **Improve Your Emotional Intelligence:** Resilient people are aware of the situation, their own emotional reactions and the behavior of those around them. In order to effectively manage feelings, it is essential to take some time to understand what is causing them and why. The more aware you are of what you are feeling, the more likely you are to maintain control of the situation and think of new ways to tackle even the most perplexing problems.

- **Realize Setbacks are Part of Life:** Resilience provides us with the capacity to deal with change and to continue to develop our potential. Because life is full of challenges, it is critical that you recalibrate your thinking of the value of hardship, heartache and hurt. Though momentarily painful, these experiences also provide invaluable opportunities to remain open, flexible, and better able to adapt to change.

- **Remember You Can Influence Outcomes:** In my view, one of the contributors to Kyle's tragic choice is he likely perceived he had lost control over what was occurring in his own life?

15

Generally, resilient people tend to have what psychologists call an *internal locus of control*. In other words, they believe their actions can and will have an effect on the outcome of an event. Of course, some factors are simply outside of our personal control, such as an earthquake, cancer diagnosis, or other tragedy. What's important is that we not lose sight of the fact we may not control the event, but we do possess the power to make choices that will affect our situation, our ability to cope, and our future.

- **Invest in developing your Problem-Solving Skills:** In today's complex, dynamic and rapidly changing world, problem-solving skills are essential. When times are tough, our minds can quickly become clouded and our vision obscured. This leads to tunnel vision, which prevents us from picking up on critical cues, important details or prevents us from taking advantage of relevant opportunities. Developing problem-solving skills enables disciplined thinking which, in turn, informs intentional action. When a crisis emerges, resilient people can quickly spot a solution that will lead to a safe outcome.

- **Commit to Being a Survivor, Not a Victim:** When dealing with any potential crisis, it is essential to view yourself as a survivor. Avoid falling into the very dangerous trap of characterizing yourself as a victim of circumstance. While the immediate situation may be unavoidable, you can still commit to staying focused on pursuing a positive outcome. Refuse to promote a pity party when adversity knocks. Choose instead to lean in when it would be far easier to fall back.

Author Hara Estroff Marano reminds us how "The heart of resilience is a belief in oneself—yet also a belief in something larger than oneself. Resilient people do not let adversity define them. They find resilience by moving towards a goal beyond themselves, transcending pain and grief by perceiving bad times as a temporary state of affairs... It's possible to strengthen your inner self and your belief in yourself, to define yourself as capable and competent. It's possible to fortify your psyche. It's possible to develop a sense of mastery."

I certainly couldn't say it any better.

It is inevitable that life will throw you some curveballs. What waits to be seen is how you choose to respond to these dynamic and often disruptive events. The moments that possess the potential to either break you or build you.

My prayer is that you will choose to be the bamboo in a hurricane, accepting that you may bend but you won't break. No matter how strong life's tempests may blow.

4

Strive to Thrive

"Our lives are the sum of the choices we make."
Albert Camus

Many citizen leaders are unable to pinpoint the exact moment they first decided to embrace the personal discomfort associated with taking action to right a wrong and change the world. Simone Honikman, however, remembers with great clarity the day she made that choice.

A doctor in Cape Town, South Africa, her first daughter had just turned one year old when she attended a conference on maternal mental health. It was 2002 and, following decades of segregation, the country was just starting to stand on its own two feet.

Although originally compelled to attend the conference because it offered an impressive array of presenters from around the world, Simone remembers being shocked to learn of the extraordinarily high rate of postnatal depression occurring in the outskirts of her own city. Not more than a dozen miles from her home, she was heartbroken to hear that a staggering 35 percent of mothers in the impoverished suburbs of Cape Town were experiencing a paralyzing sense of hopelessness at a rate that was nearly three times higher than it was in developed countries. "I was so struck," she recalls, "by the paradoxes of pain and motherhood—of deprivation and affluence. I felt compelled to do something... Not doing anything would have been intolerable."

But by her own admission, transforming the desire to accept responsibility for creating conditions for others to thrive into tangible action was daunting. After all, the need was so immense and she was unclear where she should start.

It certainly would have been understandable if Simone had chosen to leave this work to someone else perhaps better suited to such an endeavor, say a social worker, a non-governmental agency worker, or perhaps a full-time minister. But for all the reasons she could have just walked away, she chose instead to step out in faith, opting to act on this opportunity to build value into others' lives.

In a matter of weeks after attending the conference she established the Postnatal Mental Health Project (PMHP), receiving early support from the midwives and administrators of the hospital in which she worked. Starting with providing free screening for women, mostly from low-income communities, she quickly expanded into counseling and psychological services for new, primarily poor, single mothers. And her innovative approach began to pay off almost immediately.

Take the story of Gloria from Cape Town, for instance. Pregnant at 14 and worried about how she would support herself at such a young age, she suffered her first severe depression. She went on to suffer through two more depressions in later pregnancies, until she finally found PMHP. The services she received helped stabilize her situation, transforming her sense of powerlessness into a positive attitude about motherhood that equipped her to better care for her children.

Then there was Babalwe, a shy, young woman with a history of verbal and physical abuse at the hands of family members. Pregnant as a teenager and suicidal, Babalwe's depression made it difficult for her to work to support herself—until she started receiving free counseling from PMHP. Within months of visiting the clinic, and with a new-found hope in her heart, she boldly set out to create a better life for herself.

And she hasn't looked back since.

Today, more than 13,000 women and scores of children in South Africa have benefitted from PMHP's actions since its founding almost a decade ago. Their example continues to serve as a light to those trapped in the darkness of depression and mental illness. Their willingness to write a better story line for their lives can be traced back to the others-centered leader, Simone Honikman, who first set aside her own fear of change so she could help create conditions for others to flourish and thrive.

* * *

The concept of *thriving* gets to the heart of what it means to live life to its fullest. Whereas failure to thrive indicates we are depleted, unconvinced what we are doing has value, thriving means we have a growing realization of our own potential. We are stretching and moving forward—not necessarily in terms of pay or position, but in how we choose to address the opportunities set before us to make a difference in our surroundings.

Researchers in the field of positive individual and organizational change tell us that when we are thriving we are considered to be deeply satisfied, productive, and engaged in creating the future we desire. Hence, to thrive is *to routinely think more broadly about the circumstances of our lives.* It reflects an active, intentional engagement in the process of personal growth that can only come when we willingly risk abandoning the status quo in search of new horizons.

Admittedly, I'm not a psychotherapist—I don't even play one on TV—but I can comfortably predict that, be it in our homes, workplaces, worship spaces, or communities, we will encounter both good times and tough times. We can't avoid them, no matter how hard we try. The successful person, however, trains him or herself to seek out opportunities to transform our innate desire to thrive into tangible reality. How? Begin by committing to:

> **Turn off at night:** We all need time to unplug and recharge our mental, physical and spiritual batteries. Set a time every night when you quit answering the phone, checking the Blackberry

or surfing the web. Take time to invest meaningfully in you and in those around you.

Help others in need: Psychologists and sociologists continue to remind us that one of the most powerful ways to increase happiness and elevate satisfaction is to follow the example of Simone Honikman and lend a helping hand. Seek ways to set aside your agenda and actively serve someone in need. You'll find it's a win-win situation.

Rethink happiness: So many people today in our materialistic society believe happiness is a product of what we get, grab or gather for ourselves. The fact is, nothing could be farther from the truth. True happiness comes from knowing our lives have value; that we are doing something that matters; and that, as all those touched by PMHP's selfless actions demonstrate, we are doing our personal best to help make tomorrow a little better or brighter for those around us.

Invest in pursuing your passions: Passion is the fuel that moves us in the direction of our dreams. It's the propellant that compels us to see challenges as the price of achieving our potential. As my friend Angela Maiers frequently reminds me, "Passion is not only a differentiator; it is a difference maker." Passion makes the impossible possible. It's the secret sauce of the world's most effective leaders.

Vote more with your heart than your head: In a world obsessed with amassing fortunes, achieving titles and acquiring trophies, it is easy to become confused about what really matters. Remember, the only person who should define what a life well lived looks like is you. Trust your mind to inform you and allow your heart to guide you. Stay true to the real you.

Embrace opportunity: The word opportunity derives from the Greek word *topos*, the same term from which we get the English noun topography. It means territory. Hence, embracing opportunity speaks to our willingness to take new ground. It's choosing to see possibility where others only see obstacles. It is deliberately walking past our fears in pursuit of our wildest dreams and aspirations.

One of my senior Air Force mentors is fond of saying, "The best leaders don't push for revolution, but instead seek to promote evolution." In other words, they are always looking for ways to transform present circumstances, no matter how daunting, into an opportunity to stretch, grow, and ultimately, thrive.

Ready to get started?

5

Live the Golden Rule

"A man is called selfish not for pursuing his own good, but for neglecting his neighbor's."
Richard Whately

Maly's father died when she was a baby. While still a toddler, her mother became ill with tuberculosis and could no longer work. The family suddenly found themselves with no means to make ends meet, so Maly began scrounging in the local city streets.

Barely ten years old and still begging for a living, Maly came across a series of men who, instead of offering help or hope, sexually exploited her.

Shortly thereafter, she turned to child prostitution as a way to feed her ailing mother. Her mother did not know what her daughter had to go through in order to get that plate of rice on the table every evening. And young Maly, filled with guilt and shame, never told her.

Several months after her eleventh birthday, Maly was again scrounging for food when she was assaulted by several men. Physically and mentally traumatized by the brutal attack, she was subsequently institutionalized in a government facility. In short order, however, she escaped and returned to the streets. After several years, feeling increasingly worthless and lost, she became convinced no one could ever possibly love her again for who she really was.

As it turns out, she was mistaken.

Local workers for an organization called, simply, *Love146*, men and women committed to eliminating the sexual exploitation of children around the globe, found Maly and took her in. They not only provided her ailing body with food and clothing, but shared unconditional love and acceptance to nourish her broken spirit. And today, because of the willingness of a small group of ordinary leaders to live out their commitment to practicing the Golden Rule, Maly has been liberated from the horror and pain of abuse and is experiencing love as she has never known it before.

*   *   *

Think about the simplicity of the Golden Rule: "Do unto others as you would have them do unto you." Or, put even more succinctly, "*Love thy neighbor.*"

That's it.

Those three words are packed with enough power to positively influence every element of our lives. Be it our marriage, our family relationships, work relationships or friendships, putting the golden rule into practice day in and day out has the potential to transform even the most heartbreaking predicaments into hope-filled outcomes.

The Golden Rule, a positive command to show love proactively, is so effective because it challenges us to use empathy—moral imagination—to put ourselves in others' shoes. It's a simple but profoundly powerful way of thinking about our role in the world that compels us to act toward others as we would want them to act toward us.

Sadly though, The Golden Rule is all too often not part of our daily lives. In politics, business, even education and healthcare, people often tend to view such an approach as being too soft and not managerial enough. Yet nothing could be further from the truth. The fact of the matter is for thousands of years The Golden Rule has proven to be a timeless formula for adding tangible value to ones surroundings.

Here are several ways to begin making The Golden Rule less a slick slogan and more a compelling call on your life to consistently bring out the best in those around you:

Be Attentive. Recognize that we are all in this adventure called life together. When we take time to be attentive and pay attention to each other, we breathe new life into our relationships. So give someone today the undivided gift of you—your time, attention, love and compassion. It is one of the greatest treasures you can share with another human being. A gift others will cherish immensely.

Be Open. Life's greatest privilege is to become who you truly are. Becoming your best you, however, isn't something that will happen by accident. It must be intentional. So take notice of all those people who have invested kindness into your life, and pay it forward when you're able. Live The Golden Rule by opening yourself to opportunities to help others grow into their full potential.

Be Generous. One of the simplest, yet most powerful, ways to live The Golden Rule is to be generous with your praise. Commit today to make it a priority to take notice of what you like about others and speak up. Deliberately use words that build others up, seeing it as an investment in someone that doesn't cost you a thing—yet the returns can be astounding.

Be Gracious. We have a tendency to strike back when we're treated badly. This is natural. Resist that urge. The Golden Rule isn't about retaliation. It's about treating others well, despite how they treat you. Does that mean you should be a doormat? No... You have to live your truth, assert your rights, and stand your ground. But you can do so in a way that you still treat others with the respect they deserve as a fellow human being.

One cannot help but wonder how different things might be in the world today if more of us would commit to generously and unconditionally serving those around us by intentionally living The

Golden Rule. I suspect it would certainly help improve morale, heighten satisfaction and encourage greater engagement. Most importantly, however, it would help transform even the most challenging circumstances into hope-filled outcomes.

And I can prove it.

*　　*　　*

Years ago, Dr. Karl Menninger, a renowned doctor and psychologist at a psychiatric hospital, was seeking the cause of many of his patients' illnesses. One day he decided to call in his staff and proceeded to unfold a plan for developing in his clinic an atmosphere reflecting The Golden Rule. He directed all patients be given large quantities of unconditional love. No unloving attitudes were to be displayed in the presence of patients. Doctors and nurses were challenged to go about their work with a commitment to treating their neighbor (or in this case, their patient) as they themselves would like to be treated if their roles were reversed.

At the end of six months, the time spent by patients recovering from illness in the institution was cut in half!

As Dr. Menninger's experience affirms, when we make it a priority to live The Golden Rule, we enhance everyone's capacity for good. When we commit to treating others as we ourselves want to be treated, we initiate a cycle of positivity that brings out the best in ourselves and those around us, demonstrating firsthand why selflessly and intentionally loving thy neighbor has been called the crowning grace of humanity, the light of the soul, and the golden link which binds us all together.

Ask yourself how your home, workplace, worship space and community might be more invigorated and inspired if you made The Golden Rule less a slick slogan and more an intentional lifestyle choice. I suspect you will love the answer.

6

Tap Into Your Talent

"I believe that every person is born with talent."
Maya Angelou

There were once two brothers who were each given a gift. One boy, Bill, fearful his gift would be lost or stolen, chose to hide his gift under a rock to keep it safe. His brother, Dave, on the other hand, took his treasure and bought some seed.

Dave planted and cared for his seeds and soon found himself with a bountiful harvest. He routinely took his goods to a market and sold them for a very tidy profit. With his profit he bought more supplies and equipment and planted even more seeds the next season.

Bill's gift, in the meantime, remained secure under his rock.

Dave researched and implemented innovative ways to make better use of his acreage. At harvest time, he made an even bigger profit and set out to learn about supply and demand. He discovered how some goods have greater appeal to consumers and began planting the seeds that more people desired.

Dave's next harvest was the biggest yet and he chose to invest some of his money in buying better farming equipment. Due to his hard work and skill, his product began to be marketed and sold throughout the country. Dave became a very wealthy person.

Bill's gift, in the meantime, remained secure under his rock.

Dave chose not to simply accumulate his money and let it sit in a bank. Instead, he put it to work by establishing programs to help others learn how they too could use their gifts in ways that would make the world around them better than they first found it. Dave then built a school that taught business and economics and formed a charitable organization that would help others far and wide benefit from his original gift.

Meanwhile, Bill, who was now a man, still had his original gift. It was safely hidden under the same rock. While his brother grew to become very successful, blessing the lives of countless others with his gift, Bill's life seemed stagnant and small. With his gift hidden from view, he risked little and achieved less, falling far short of ever really knowing how things may have been different if he too had chosen to do as his brother and use his gift to wilfully build tangible value into his surroundings.

*   *   *

As this modern day Parable of the Talents is designed to remind us, we all possess unique gifts, talents, and skills meant to be used to help make our part of the world better than we first found it. When we make it a priority to do as Dave in our story and generously share our natural abilities, everyone benefits. Conversely, when we choose to do as Bill and hide or hoard our talents, everyone loses.

Unfortunately, instead of seeing talent as merely the unique contribution we all have to share with the world, it's common to associate talent only with a celebrated few. We look at someone like LeBron James swaying and knifing his way to the basket, and marvel at his brilliance. Deep down, we know the secret weapon of his success is his talent, a talent he employs liberally to the fascination of anyone who watches him play.

In the same way millions of people marvel at LeBron's incredible talent, we look to a host of other celebrities—Al Pacino, Tiger Woods, Michael Phelps, Adele Adkins and Julia Roberts—for example, and we think the same thing: they possess incredible talent. They are blessed with an amazing gift. For most of us, then, such talent seems a rare and precious thing, bestowed on a small handful of special, far-away people. They are different, these people with talent. They are "not us."

I beg to differ.

Instead of adopting such a narrow, specialized understanding of talent, how would things be different in the world if we viewed talent as less a matter of genetic disposition and more a reflection of purposeful determination? The emphasis here is on the word 'purposeful'.

Be it your fascination with building businesses, your passion for serving others, or your commitment to exploring, questioning and recreating the current state of affairs, putting your talent to work is about intentionally and productively leveraging your natural strengths to make a positive difference in your surroundings. It's choosing to liberally share the best of you with everyone around you.

At the same time, developing the talent of those around you should be viewed as positive leadership job one. After all, no sophisticated solution can be developed, superior product designed, sensational service delivered,, or collective progress achieved, if as leaders we fail to create conditions for the talent in our midst to flourish and thrive. So with these thoughts in mind, how can you get busy unlocking the unique talent within yourself and those around you? Begin by seeking out opportunities to:

> **Tap into creative leanings and natural inclinations**. By feeding and answering the call to apply oneself in new and novel ways, we improve the quality of our own life while concurrently enriching the lives of those around us. Conversely, denying ourselves the opportunity to stretch outside our comfort zones in the direction of our dreams can lead to stagnation and frustration. In the words of a former boss, Major General Winfield Scott III, "Don't be afraid to set off into unfamiliar territory. Make a plan, set a direction, then move out and be ready to take fire. You and your team will be better for it."

Tap into the potential to create something of beauty or significance. Jim Elliot once shared, "He is no fool who gives what he cannot keep to gain which he cannot lose." What he is speaking of is the reality that too many people only dream about what could be instead of using their talents to materialize a solution. When you get busy transforming your natural talents into a tangible form that can be enjoyed, experienced and shared by others, everyone wins.

Tap into your original, best you. All of us possess the ability to do something nobody else can. We all have a special strength capable of adding immense value to our surroundings. "If you were meant to cure cancer or write a symphony or crack cold fusion and you don't," asserts author Steve Pressfield in *The War of Art*, "you not only hurt yourself, even destroy yourself; you hurt your children. You hurt me. You hurt the planet." Doing your best work is not a selfish act or a bid for attention on the part of the actor. It's a gift to the world and every being in it. Don't cheat humanity of your one-of-a kind contribution. Generously give all you've got and trust that everyone you encounter will be the grateful you did.

Each of us is born with talents that we are free to share or to hide. When we liberally offer our best selves to others, we foster growth, enhance happiness and promote posterity. And as a result, the world literally becomes a different place. However, when we choose to hide our talents, we deny everyone the opportunity to experience us at our peak, positive performance.

Don't cheat those around you. Give the world the best of what's inside you. Tap into your talent and do what only you can.

Why not give it a try, beginning today?

7

Believe the Best in Yourself

*"When you doubt your power, you
give power to your doubt."*
Honore de Balzac

Visualize you are an ice skater in a competition. You are in first place going into the final round. If you perform well, the gold medal is yours. You are nervous, anxious and frightened.

Then, mere minutes before it's your turn to take the ice, your trainer rushes over to you with incredible news: "You've already won! The judges tabulated the scores, and none of the skaters can possibly catch up with you. You are too far ahead to lose."

Upon hearing that news, how do you feel? Relieved, thankful, exhilarated!

Whereas a moment ago self-doubt and fear of falling short dominated your thoughts, now you are filled with a new found courage, confidence and sense of belief in yourself. So how do you choose to skate your final performance? Will you be timid? Cautious? Will you play it extra safe? Of course not. You will go all out to be and do your best because the prize is already yours.

You will skate like a champion because that is what you are.

* * *

Although you may not be an ice skater, you get my point. Often in life, the greatest hindrance to achieving our dreams and attaining our potential is us. Specifically, it is our inability to overcome the limiting beliefs that seek to have us doubt all we are capable of being and doing.

We experience this as the voice in our head that says:

You can't do it.

You'll never be good enough.

You're going to fail.

This voice of self-doubt strives to convince us we are incapable of achieving an ambitious goal. It criticizes us when life gets difficult. It beats us down when we struggle to stand up against its running demoralizing and disempowering commentary.

Intuitively, we all know we should not let self-doubt bother us. But like an elusive enemy, it frequently manages to slip right on past our defenses.

As I've discovered so many times in my own life and leadership journey, self-doubt is a challenging adversary. When it's loose, it devours confidence, strips reason from our mind, and steals happiness from our heart. In return, it leaves us feeling fearful, insecure and questioning our abilities. And perhaps worst of all, it seems as though the more you fight your self-doubt, the more it seems to fight back.

So how can we proactively position ourselves to diminish the power self-doubt has over our lives? What proven, practical steps can we take to think and act in ways that affirms our belief the prize is already ours for the taking? Begin by committing to:

> **Live your Truth**: Your personal truth represents the values and beliefs that guide how you lead your life. You may value development, personal health or wealth, community, honesty, or business success. When you believe deeply in what you're doing and align your words and your ways appropriately, you are tapping into your reservoir of deepest potential. On the other hand, when your actions are at odds with your personal sense of truth, you will quickly lose faith in yourself at the

first stumble, setback, or sign of rejection, and self-doubt will continue to have its way with you.

Align your choices with your intentions: Your intentions are the desired results of your actions; they are your goals. If you have internalized your goals and are consistently making choices that support attaining them, it's much easier to be motivated to face your doubts, fears and frustrations head-on … regardless how nerve-racking your present circumstances.

Build a Network: It is virtually impossible to achieve our greatest dreams and aspirations alone. Life is, after all, a team sport. If you don't take tangible steps to share your desires with others, you will miss out on the valuable experience, ideas and encouragement others have to offer. Make it a priority to build a network of people who can accompany you in the journey. Always keep in mind it is easier to believe in yourself when you share your purpose and progress with people who are on a related path.

Tell yourself you can: Psychologists have been reminding us for years that we are each 'architects of our own realities', and they are absolutely right. The way we think about our potential has a significant impact on how we feel about ourselves and how willing we are to stay the course when facing challenging or uncomfortable situations. If you tell yourself you can't do it, it's likely that you won't. Telling yourself you can, on the other hand, helps make success a self-fulfilling prophecy.

Stop listening to toxic people: Toxic people, those negative individuals we encounter in life who prefer to focus more on problems than orient to possibilities, are often quick to shoot down our ideas and diminish our desires. You know the type. You see white, they say black; you seek the good, they lament the bad;

you seek opportunity, they are intent on fixating on obstacles; you strive to build on the best of what is and they refuse to move past the worst of how things are. In a nutshell, toxic people steal our joy, zap our energy and constrain us from attaining our potential. They'll try to lead you into a state of hopelessness.

Don't let them do it.

Choose to surround yourself with supportive and passionate people who can both inspire you and bring out the best in you. Align yourself with optimistic people who possess the moral courage not to sugar coat present reality—those who will lift you up when you feel down and help you see the bright side of your darkest fears and overcome your most debilitating self-doubts when the challenges before you seem overwhelming.

Remember, feelings of self-doubt never disappear. They are always lurking in the shadows of your mind, ready to greet you every time you step out of your comfort zone. You can choose, however, to set aside your momentary doubts and move out in the direction of your dreams and desires. Resolve to believe you are ready and able to give your best performance to whatever it is you are doing, and you will soon discover for yourself you are already a champion—simply for having given your best effort in that moment.

8

Discover Your Unique Value

"Happiness is your own treasure because it lies within you."
Prem Rawat

Over three hundred years ago, the Burmese army planned to invade Thailand. At the time, Thailand was known as Siam. Hearing of the impending attack, Siamese monks at a large monastery were determined to protect their shrine and the prized object it contained: an amazing 10 foot high solid gold Buddha statue. While it was priceless to them for reasons that transcend money, the monks knew the Burmese soldiers would stop at nothing to steal the statue because of its tremendous value.

The monks quickly covered the Golden Buddha with 12 inches of clay knowing that the foreign invaders would totally ignore it and think it worthless. Sadly, the members of the monastery were slaughtered in the ensuing attack and the secret of the Golden Buddha stayed hidden for two hundred years.

In the mid 1950s, the government of Thailand set out to relocate the monastery to make room for a new highway. The resident monks arranged for a crane to come and move the clay Buddha to a new location. However, when the crane started to lift the statue, it was much heavier than expected and it began to crack. Wanting to protect the ancient shrine, the monks ordered the crane operator to lower the statue back to the ground as they awaited the arrival of more powerful equipment.

That evening, a torrential monsoon rain descended on the area. So the local monks lovingly and painstakingly set out to cover the statue with tarps to keep the moisture away. In the dark of night, with the rain still raging, the lead monk took his flashlight and went out to ensure the Buddha was adequately covered. When the light of his flashlight shone into a crack in the clay, he saw a glimmer ... a reflection of something of potential value buried beneath the shroud of clay.

In order to find the source of the reflection, he started carefully chiseling away shards of clay. The more clay he proceeded to chip away, the brighter the glimmer grew. Hours later, and with all the clay removed, the stunned monk stood speechless in the presence of a massive Buddha made of solid gold.

Today, the statue resides in The Temple of the Golden Buddha in Bangkok, Thailand. Weighing in excess of 6 tons and valued at over $200 million dollars, it is the largest solid gold statue in the world. And to think such an amazing treasure was buried there all those years—invisible in plain sight—but no one knew it.

*   *   *

I believe we are all a lot like this one-time clay covered statue. Our real value is inside us. The internal treasure of our true potential remains hidden from view, unless we are willing to chip away our common way of living to reveal the golden future waiting to be shared with those around us.

Here are five self-improvement ideas to consider if you want your true value to be known to the world.

> **Remind yourself you have immense power:** Settling for less than we are capable of being or doing, or staying right where we are indefinitely, won't get us very far. We each possess the power to make our days more productive and enjoyable

simply by realizing that where we are is a great place to begin intentionally in the direction we want to be.

Ask yourself, "Am I satisfied with the direction I am currently going?"

Conquer Yourself: Keep in mind that being true to yourself is the foundation of happiness and success in life. Knowing yourself is the foundation of wisdom. Pushing yourself builds a foundation for success. It is more important to conquer yourself in these ways than it is to win dozens of battles elsewhere in life.

Ask yourself, "Am I acting consistent with my values? Am I pursuing my path, or a path someone has prescribed for me?"

Expect Speed Bumps: The path to success is littered with missteps and mistakes. Avoiding them is impossible. What will ultimately define your success or failure won't be the number of challenges and difficulties you encounter, but rather, how you choose to respond to them.

Ask yourself, "Am I responding to life's speed bumps and hurdles in ways that enable me to grow into my full potential?"

Resolve to Make a Difference: All of us want to lead lives of meaning and significance. Commit to doing what you do because you believe it's the right thing to do. Be a difference maker.

Ask yourself, "Am I doing what I can to leave the world a little better than I found it?"

Our daily lives overflow with opportunities to learn, grow, develop our strengths, and move forward. Every day provides a new opportunity to allow our very best self to see the light of day. But it is up to each of us to do the work required to reveal our potential to those around us.

Don't keep such an amazing treasure buried, invisible in plain sight. Resolve today to use your talents, gifts and skills to add unique value to your surroundings.

No torrential monsoon rain required to get started.

9

Always Invest in Relationships

"The meeting of two personalities is like the
contact of two chemical substances: if there
is any reaction, both are transformed."
C.G. Jung

On January 3, 1864, the *Grafton*, an English schooner piloted by Captain Thomas Musgrave, was destroyed by a hurricane that broke its anchor chains and sunk on the rocky beach on the southern end of Auckland Island. The captain and his crew of four men made it to shore but not to safety. Auckland Island, after all, is one of the most inhospitable places on earth, with freezing rain, howling winds, and little to eat year round. On May 10th of the same year, the *Invercauld*, an Aberdeen clipper piloted by Captain George Dalgarno, was struck by a heavy gale and driven between two steep cliffs on the northern side of Auckland Island and sunk. Nineteen of the twenty-five men aboard the *Invercauld* made it ashore, unaware that the survivors of the *Grafton*'s crew were living on the other side of the island.

The survivors of the *Grafton* chose to abandon formalities and adopted group problem solving and decision making. Conversely, the survivors of the *Invercauld* retained the formal hierarchy that served them so well on the high seas. Although the challenges to survive were quite similar, the outcomes for these two crews could not have been more different. The crew of the *Grafton* worked together to find food and water, consulted with and looked after one another, constructed shelter, and contributed to their rescue by building a vessel and setting out to sea where they were found by Captain Cross of the *Flying Scud*. The crew of the *Invercauld*, on the other hand, fought and bickered, lost 16 of the 19 crewmembers to cold or hunger, descended into cannibalism and, ultimately, the three remaining survivors were found only by chance.

For all the talk today about the power of inclusion, collaboration, flattening organizations, and valuing everyone's strength and potential contribution, there are still many leaders who are hesitant to let go of the 'command and control' mindset. You know the type. They are in charge, you're not, and what they say goes. Everyone has their place in the hierarchy and theirs is at the top. After all, they've earned it. They've paid their dues, done their time, and now they get to issue orders.

The results of such leaders' unwillingness to share power, set aside their self-interest and engage those around them in the process of pursuing a collective purpose, speak for themselves:

- – Productivity plummets;
- – Creativity collapses;
- – Dependence dissipates;
- – And people are left feeling as though they must fend for themselves.

What's the remedy? Strive to build a team with a common purpose, shared performance goals, and a keen sense of mutual accountability for outcomes. Begin by:

- **Establishing Clear Expectations**: People can only flourish and thrive when they possess a keen understanding of what is expected of them. Communicating clear expectations squeezes out ambiguity, enhances clarity, and dramatically reduces opportunities for misunderstanding.

- **Promoting understanding** of why a group of diverse people need to be a team. You accomplish this by helping everyone understand the team's goals and communicating what each team member contributes to the team's overall success.
- **Facilitating effective interaction** in such a way as to ensure good problem solving, decision making and coordination of effort.
- **Ensuring the team has adequate knowledge** to accomplish its task. This includes information relevant to the team's goals and individual job competencies.
- **Establishing common goals** that are simple, measurable and clearly relevant to the team's task. Understanding and working toward these common goals as a unit is crucial to the team's effectiveness.
- **Making collaboration a core competency.** In effective teams you'll notice a strong desire to collaborate and a keen awareness of interdependency. Focusing on collaboration and interdependency will increase commitment by defusing blaming behavior and stimulating opportunities for learning and growth.

A person's ability to make things happen in and through others depends entirely on their ability to lead them. Without effective leadership, there is no cohesion or teamwork and people go their own way. If you want to pursue a big dream, mission or cause, then you must persuade others to go with you.

Remember, a willingness to participate collaboratively as a team member does not guarantee an easy journey. However, as the success of the *Grafton* crew demonstrates firsthand, when a leader is willing to create an environment in which everyone on the team is intent on looking after one another, contribute to a shared purpose, and selflessly serve those around them, anything is possible—even if one day you find yourself stranded on one of the most inhospitable places on earth, with freezing rain, howling winds, and little to eat year round.

10

Pursue a Powerful Purpose

"You have everything you need to build
something far bigger than yourself."
Seth Godin

As a lifelong student of leadership, I spend a lot of time seeking out ideas, opinions and perspectives that stretch my understanding and challenge my assumptions about what it takes to enhance my effectiveness and maximize my influence. One of the philosophers I've come across in my journey of continual exploration is Ayn Rand. I'm particularly fond of this quote:

> *"Man's mind is his basic tool of survival. Life is given to him, survival is not. His body is given to him, its sustenance is not. His mind is given to him, its content is not. To remain alive he must act and before he can act he must know the nature and purpose of his actions."*

I think the reason these words resonate so deeply with me is that they highlight something common to each of us; namely, all of us long to know we are leading lives of purpose, meaning and significance. Though no two people's journeys are exactly alike, we all strive to make our mark on the world.

We want our presence to be felt.

We need to know we've made a difference.

The challenge, however, is that, in the process of moving through the journey we call life, it's easy to allow our uniqueness to be crowded out. Yes, I said allow. After all, no one can tell us how to lead our lives. Sure, they can make demands. They can levy expectations, and they can even try to forcefully inject their opinions and ideals about the path we should take. Make no mistake about it; we are the only ones who can decide which path we ultimately follow. Only we can choose to stay true to the deepest longings of our heart. Only we can choose to quit focusing on our limitations and continue to pursue the dreams and aspirations born of our imaginations.

However, breakthroughs in neuroimaging technology reveal that as we age, the center of cognitive gravity tends to shift from the imaginative right brain to the logical left brain. The particular challenge with this phenomenon is that it illuminates our natural tendency to live more out of our memory than we do our imaginations. In other words, unless we willfully take tangible steps to consistently create the future we desire, our dreams will fade and our influence will shrink in proportion.

So what can we do to help keep our imaginations alive and stay on track to reach our full, positive potential? I recommend developing what I term *a personal purpose statement*.

A personal purpose statement is a simple yet important step in aligning our attitudes with our actions. It's what puts steel in our spine when we find ourselves facing choices that are inconvenient, uncomfortable, or just plain unsettling. It's what gives us the strength to persevere when doubts are high and confidence is low. Perhaps most importantly, it serves as a compass we can count on to lead us through the twists and turns of life in a way that protects us from ending up too far from our desired destination.

For the sake of giving you a deeper understanding of what I'm describing, I've listed my own personal purpose statement below. I try to look at it every morning as I spend a few minutes in quiet reflection, preparing to launch into the new day:

> *Every day I will be thankful for the many blessings that surround me;*
> *I will keep my feet moving along the path set before me;*
> *My hands busy with the opportunities provided me;*
> *My heart open to serving those around me; and*
> *My eyes focused on eternity.*

As you can see, such a statement doesn't have to be lengthy. Nor does it have to be complex. What's important is that you take the time to capture in a few, brief sentences the thoughts which will ultimately equip you to make choices that are consistent with your values instead of merely convenient to your situation.

Please keep in mind that you cannot lead well merely by copying others. To make your unique mark on the world you must know the nature and purpose of the actions you plan to take. After all, leadership is a personal expression of who you are, inside and out. It's a reflection to others of what you are willing to fight for in your life and it begins by having a definite understanding of your purpose.

As I wrap up, I have two quick questions for you.

- Do you know what purpose, cause or campaign you are willing to pursue with relentless commitment and determination?
- Have you taken the time to reflect and capture your personal purpose statement?

If the answer to either of these questions is no, then let me encourage you to take some time to explore how you can better share your true you, your best you, with those around you by developing a personal purpose statement. I think you'll find it will not only improve your leadership effectiveness, it will also multiply your influence, increase your satisfaction, and enhance your ability to lead a life of true meaning and significance—one purposeful act at a time.

11

Stay True to You

"Honesty is the cornerstone of all success, without which
confidence and ability to perform shall cease to exist."
Mary Kay Ash

In 1970, Dr. Anthony Downs, a real estate finance expert, was working for his father when approached by Mayor Richard J. Daley of Chicago. At the time, Mayor Daley was considered the most powerful mayor in America and he was in political trouble.

It turns out his hand-picked county assessor had been accused of reducing the assessed values of large properties in the city in return for sizable campaign contributions. The mayor was concerned that if this accusation turned out to be true, it could undermine his upcoming reelection campaign. So he hired the prominent real estate research firm owned by Dr. Downs's father to analyze the assessor's office and implement any necessary reforms.

Downs specifically recalls how on the first day of this highly visible assignment, Mayor Daley put his arm around him and said, "Do the job right, even if you have to fire everybody in the Assessor's Office." Little did the mayor realize how he'd come to later regret those words.

As Downs began to comb through the records of the Assessor's Office, it became very clear it was a disaster. Dishonesty was rampant. And the deeper Downs dug, the uglier it became.

The office's top people were aging bureaucrats who continued to use obsolete methods that systematically over-valued property in the city's poorest neighborhoods and undervalued it in the wealthiest ones, causing severe and unjust assessments to be levied on those struggling to make ends meet.

Among other things, he found the assessment ratios used in the Mayor's and Assessor's own wards, and the ratio of assessed values to true market values were half the levels of those in the rest of the county. Therefore, to ensure fairness, Downs and his team were going to have to recommend doubling the property tax rates, and thus the taxes, in the mayor's own neighborhood. When Mayor Daley found out about this plan, he was furious and demanded that no such thing be done. Downs, however, staying true to his word to "do the job right", pressed on and saw that the mayor's taxes were raised anyway.

Shortly thereafter, Mayor Daley ordered the city not to hire Dr. Downs's firm again. And they didn't. Although the loss of the lucrative city contract resulted in hundreds of thousands of dollars in lost revenue, to this day, Downs confirms he wouldn't do anything different.

What's the lesson from this story for the rest of us?

Sooner or later, you are going to run into your own versions of Mayor Daley. Whether it's as a leader, follower, parent, or citizen, you will be tempted or pressured to bend the truth and contribute to perpetuating a lie. It could be as simple as knowingly walking by a situation you know is wrong and refusing to intercede. Or, it could be refusing to stand up and fighting for those who cannot fight for themselves when you become aware of a situation that is unjust, unfair, or outright inappropriate.

Truth is a fundamental value and an honorable pursuit. We all yearn for truth. Scientists search for it every day. All good relationships and reputations are built on truth. Committing to telling the truth, especially when you know it will likely result in repercussions against you, is not easy. But as the Greek philosopher, Epictetus, once said, "If you seek truth you will not seek victory by dishonorable means, and if you find truth, you will become invincible."

Wherever you are called to lead and serve today, commit to stand for truth...remembering it is something that should begin at home, should be natural at work, and is something people appropriately expect and naturally demand from the leaders in their lives.

Truth is a precious gift. Steward it well. Begin today by staying true to you. No matter who may try to persuade or pressure to do otherwise.

12

Choose Commitment
Over Involvement

*"Kamikaze pilots are only useful if they are committed
to their mission. Leaders are the same way. You
cannot have involvement without commitment
and be effective. It goes with the territory."*
Dr. Tim Elmore

I love the story Tim Elmore shares of the WWII Japanese kamikaze pilot who was interviewed by a local news reporter upon returning from his 50th mission. The reporter noted that the kamikaze pilot was a contradiction in terms. After all, how could someone be a kamikaze pilot and still be alive after 50 missions? Aren't they supposed to give their life in the process of fighting the enemy? Yet, there he stood, alive and well.

"Here's the reality," the kamikaze pilot responded. "I am very involved in what I do. Not very committed, mind you, but very involved."

I can't help but chuckle every time I think about this story As an aviator myself, I am keenly aware of the fact that a true kamikaze pilot only makes a single flight. They are expected to give their life for their mission. As Tim Elmore likes to say, "There is no such thing as a half-hearted kamikaze. Commitment goes with the territory."

So it should be with each of us.

Unfortunately, the world today is filled with half-hearted kamikaze pilots who routinely fail to live up to commitments. Every day, balls get dropped, deadlines are skipped, deliveries are missed, promises are broken, and well-intended initiatives don't get accomplished. And it's easy to see why. In an age of increasing demands, an avalanche of information, and a virtual explosion in technology and communication, why are we surprised that personal accountability is becoming more diluted and keeping our commitments more challenging than ever?

In my opinion, the failure to follow through is one of the (if not the) primary challenge facing our businesses, our marriages, our communities, and our nation. We are quick to say we believe in something, then drift away from it. We don't hesitate to promise something then fall away from it at the slightest hint of trouble or tribulation. The fact of the matter is, talk is cheap and half-hearted kamikazes are a dime a dozen. What the world needs are more positive, others-centered leaders who are unafraid to make and keep commitments.

"But how?" you ask.

It's simple, but not easy. Get started by following these three practical tips:

> **Keep it simple**: Leonardo da Vinci once said, "Simplicity is the ultimate sophistication." Nothing could be closer to the truth. In a world where expectations and demands can get the best of anyone, the most effective way to cut through the clutter is to simplify. One of the easiest ways to do this is to guard yourself from starting too many projects at once. No one, no matter how talented, can consistently deliver on their commitments if they are oversubscribed As a rule of thumb, consider keeping your attention channeled to no more initiatives than you can count on one hand at any given time.

> **Negotiate clear agreements**: One of the biggest impediments to keeping our commitments is unclear expectations, murky

timelines, and ill-defined responsibilities. Guard yourself from falling into this trap by clarifying what you're going to do (and not do) right up front. If you are unable to deliver on schedule, make a timely counter-promise to those depending on you that you can keep. If you find yourself unable to fulfill a commitment altogether, have the courage to tell those impacted you cannot deliver.

Practice the Nice "No": As human beings, we are natural pleasers. We want people to like us and we want to fit in. Although there is nothing wrong with this reality, the fact is we find it much easier to say yes than we do no, making it all-too-easy to routinely over commit and under deliver. Instead of making more commitments than you could possible complete, learn to practice what I term the Nice No. That is, resolve to be honest. Don't be afraid to tell them when you don't have the time or bandwidth to do anything else in the present, but you would be happy to reconsider in the future.

Leading well begins and ends with being someone who follows through on their commitments. The more people understand you can be counted on to deliver, that you're someone who takes their commitments seriously, the greater your influence and impact.

Remember, the world is filled with half-hearted kamikazes. What we need are more men and women who understand the value of commitment, not merely involvement. This is essential to becoming a leaders worth following. Are you up to the challenge?

13

Win the Heart

"There are powers inside of you which, if you could discover and use, would make of you everything you ever dreamed or imagined you could become."
Orison Swett Marsden

One of my favorite old stories tells about three soldiers who trudged down a road in a strange country. Returning from many years at war, they were tired, hungry and homesick. In fact, they had not slept or eaten for two days.

"How I would like a good dinner tonight," said the first.

"And a bed to sleep in," said the second.

"I too would enjoy such things," said the third. "But we must march on."

So on they marched.

Suddenly, ahead of them they began to make out the lights of a village.

"Maybe we'll find something to eat there," said the first.

"And a loft to sleep in," said the second.

"There is certainly no harm in asking," said the third.

Now the peasants in that village feared strangers, especially soldiers. When they heard that three men were coming down the road, they began whispering among themselves.

"Here come three soldiers. Soldiers are always hungry. But we have little enough for ourselves." And they hurried to hide their food.

Some pushed their sacks of barley under the hay in the lofts. Others lowered buckets of milk down the wells.

They spread old blankets over the carrot bins and hid their cabbages and potatoes inside cabinets and under beds and hung their sides of beef in the darkest recesses of their cellars.

They hid all they had to eat—then they waited.

The soldiers stopped first at the house of Jacques and Françoise.

"Good evening to you," the soldiers said. "Could you spare a bit of food and a place for three hungry and tired soldiers to briefly rest?"

"We have not eaten for three days," said Jacques. Françoise, sporting the saddest look she could muster, added, "It has been a poor harvest."

The three soldiers thanked them and went on to the house of Renaurt and Louise.

"Could we bother you for a few morsels of food? And have you some corner where we could sleep for the night?"

"I'm sorry," replied Renaurt. "We gave everything we could spare to soldiers who came before you."

"Our beds are already full," added Louise.

At Vincent and Marie's the answer was the same. It had been a poor harvest and all the grain must be kept for seed.

So it went for the soldiers as they traveled from house to house all through the village. Not one person had any food to spare or an extra bed to share.

The three soldiers conferred for a moment and then the first soldier called out, "Good people of the village!" The peasants drew near.

"As you know, we are three hungry and tired soldiers in a strange land. We have asked you for food and you have no food. We have asked for a bed and you have no beds. Well then, we will simply ask for your assistance in helping us make stone soup."

The peasants stared. Others scratched their heads. What is this strange concoction called stone soup, they wondered? That would be something to know about.

"First, we'll need a large iron pot," the soldiers said.

The peasants brought the largest pot they could find.

"Perfect," said the soldiers. "And now water to fill it and a fire to heat it."

It took many buckets of water to fill the pot. A fire was built on the village square and the pot was set to boil.

"And now, if you please, we need three round, smooth stones."

Those were easy enough to find.

The peasants' eyes grew round with wonder as they watched the soldiers drop the stones into the pot.

"Any decent soup needs salt and pepper," said the soldiers, as they began to stir the stones in the slowly boiling pot.

Several children ran to fetch salt and pepper.

"Stones like these generally make extraordinary soup. But oh, if there were a few carrots, it would be much better."

"Why, I think I have a carrot or two," said Françoise, and off she ran.

She came back with her apron full of carrots from the bin beneath the red quilt.

"The best stone soup should also have cabbage," said the soldiers as they sliced the carrots into the pot. "But no use asking for what you don't have."

"I think I could find a cabbage or two somewhere," said Marie and she hurried home. Back she came with three cabbages she had hidden under the bed.

"Now if only we only had a bit of beef and a few potatoes, this soup would be good enough for a rich man's table."

The villagers remembered their potatoes hidden inside of cabinets and sides of beef hanging in the cellars. They ran to fetch them.

The fact these simple villagers could partake of a rich man's soup—and all from a few stones—seemed like magic to them all!

"Ah," sighed the soldiers as they stirred in the beef and potatoes, "If we only had a little barley and a cup or two of milk! This would transform this soup into a delicacy fit for a king. In fact, he asked for just such a soup when last he dined with us."

The villagers looked at each other. The soldiers had entertained the king?

"But—no use asking for what you don't have," the soldiers sighed.

Several villagers virtually ran to their homes, returning with barley from their lofts and milk from their wells. The soldiers stirred the barley and milk into the steaming broth while the villagers stared.

At last the magical stone soup was ready.

"All of you shall taste," the soldiers said. "But first a suitable table must be set."

Great tables were placed in the square. And all around were lighted torches.

Such a soup! How good it smelled! Truly fit for a king.

But then several of the villagers asked themselves, "Would not such a magnificent soup require bread—and maybe even a little ale or cider?" Soon a banquet was spread and everyone sat down to eat.

Never in the history of the village had there been such a feast.

Never before had the peasants tasted such soup. Especially soup made from stones.

The villagers and soldiers ate and drank and ate and drank. And after that they danced and sang.

They danced and sang far into the night.

At last they were tired. Then the three soldiers asked, "Is there not a loft where we could sleep?"

"Let three such wise and splendid gentlemen sleep in a loft? Indeed! They must have the best beds in the village," various villagers exclaimed.

So the first soldier slept in the priest's house.

The second soldier slept in the baker's house.

And the third soldier slept in the mayor's house.

In the morning, the whole village gathered in the square to give them a warm send-off.

"Many thanks for what you have taught us," the villagers said to the soldiers. "We shall never go hungry, now that we know how to make soup from stones."

"Oh, it's all in knowing how," said the soldiers, and off they went down the road, rucksacks filled with enough provisions to see them safely home.

*   *   *

Though I have to admit I've never tried to make stone soup, I strive to do my part anywhere and everywhere I can to create the same positive effect the three soldiers had on the villagers; namely, to help others discover the value of becoming fully engaged in creating something meaningful, rewarding, and personally and professionally fulfilling.

Of course, encouraging those around us to contribute to the mission, cause, or campaign is no easier a task today than it was for the soldiers in our stone soup story. In fact, despite companies spending over $720 million each year on improving employee engagement, employee engagement is at record lows — 13% according to perennial engagement survey leader Gallup. What's wrong here? Perhaps human resource leaders are spending their money in the wrong places. Or the modern workforce is demanding more. Either way, our models and surveys aren't working, and we're making very little progress.

Sadly, too many leaders in today's workplaces continue to mistakenly believe the "soft stuff" will derail their efforts to achieve the organization's goals – yet nothing could be further from reality. It is only a fully engaged workforce that allows an organization to achieve its full potential. The fact of the matter is, the path to superior performance doesn't start in the head, merely by hiring and promoting those with the highest IQ. Rather, others-centered leaders recognize sustained organizational excellence always comes from the heart of every person on the team. As the soldiers in our story understood, capturing the hearts of the villagers by intentionally enlisting them in the journey was the key to accomplishing something together that

55

is far more significant than what any one person could ever hope of achieving alone.

In his book, *Crossing the Unknown Sea*, corporate poet David Whyte tells of a conversation he had with a trusted counselor, who made the following statement, "The antidote to exhaustion is not necessarily rest." Whyte inquired, "What is it then?" The counselor replied, "The antidote to exhaustion is wholeheartedness." He went on to explain how one grows weary because he or she fails to be fully engaged in what they are doing.

As you think about your organization, would you describe your employees as fully involved, halfheartedly going through the motions, or outright checked out of the proverbial game? Do you sense there is widespread low satisfaction, collective fatigue, and a general malaise about accomplishing the mission? If so, here are several ways you can win the hearts of your people by being a spark of positivity or inspiration to those on your team:

> **Be a Reliable Source of Support:** The closest thing to being cared for is to care for others. Awash in an impersonal world that can often make us feel invisible, we all yearn for leaders who will make a genuine attempt to connect with us at the deepest level. Think about the people who have had the greatest positive effect on your life – the ones who truly made a difference? Odds are they aren't the ones that tried to give you all the answers or solve all your problems. Instead, they're likely the ones who sat silently with you when you needed a moment to think, who provided a shoulder to lean on when you needed to cry, and who laughed and celebrated with you when things were going your way. Be this person for those around you every chance you get.
>
> **Be an Enabler of Others' Unique Potential:** One of life's greatest desires is to become who you truly are – to grow into your full, positive potential. Achieving this goal demands we

dare to be authentic selves, however anxious or odd that self may prove to be to others. The leaders in our lives who support us in operating this way are extraordinarily rare. Many people, often without realizing what they are doing or saying, are prone to recreate others in their own image. Don't let that be you.

The most effective leaders let people define themselves. They don't criticize others for being different or project their close-minded definition of how they believe people should lead their lives. Nor do they routinely prescribe the exact approach or path someone must take to achieve their objectives. Effective leaders provide clear expectations and appropriate guidelines on what is required for that person to succeed, then they step out of their way and watch them go.

Be Appreciative of Others' Contributions: The most effective leaders makes it a priority to recognize, liberate and celebrate the strength of others. They give genuine praise whenever possible, recognizing how doing so is a mighty act of service. They appreciate the value of taking a moment to pass along a genuine word of praise, be it in public or private. They understand that taking the time to reward those who are setting an example worth emulating is one of the greatest investments they can ever make.

Be More Intentional with Your Questions: Take a hard look at what you're asking your employees. If all your employee surveys and other well-intentioned interventions are focused only on work, expand the questions to understand what your people are passionate about outside work. Strive to better understand the broader influences in your people's lives like their internal values as well as the more granular issues like family needs, professional aspirations, and personal interests.

Be Tough on Results, But Gracious with People: The most effective leaders are those who create a respectful balance between achieving objectives and serving people. They appreciate that setting high standards is necessary to achieve sustainable growth and progress. They understand the value of expecting quality and excellence and holding people accountable to realistic results. They don't, however, ever treat others unprofessionally or disrespectfully when people fall short of expectations. Instead, they balance tough with gentle, and teach others through their actions.

As leaders in our homes, workplaces, worship spaces and communities, we would be wise to remember we are each capable of doing something that adds immense value to our surroundings. We each can contribute to creating conditions for mutual engagement and shared success by developing a fuller appreciation of the profoundly positive potential that comes to fruition when everyone is encouraged to bring their full, best selves to support a mission, cause, or campaign larger than themselves.

Remember, there is no greater power than a group of united hearts. Throughout history, they have built companies, won championships, decisively defeated adversaries, and established new nations. Why not commit to fully engaging not only the minds of your employees, but their hearts as well. Make it a priority to win over those you serve and I believe you will be very pleasantly surprised by what you achieve.

Stone soup optional.

ENCOURAGE

Others-centered leaders understand that how and what they communicate impacts people's performance. Knowing this, they express enthusiastic confidence in other's ability to accomplish something meaningful. They willingly promote hope and encourage those around them to push the bounds of their potential. They make others feel valued, relevant, and significant.

14

Be a Blessing

*"Do the right thing. It will gratify some
people and astonish the rest."*
Mark Twain

There once was an elderly carpenter who, after many years of successfully building homes, decided he was ready to retire. So on a Monday morning, he approached his employer and told him his intentions to leave the house building business. He shared how he now wanted to live a more leisurely life with his wife and extended family. Although he acknowledged he would miss the paycheck, he felt that he needed to retire.

It was his time to go.

The company's owner, himself an accomplished builder, was sorry to see his good worker go and asked if the carpenter could build just one more house as a personal favor. Reluctantly, the carpenter said yes, but in time, it became obvious his heart was no longer in his work. He showed up every day but his work became sloppier and sloppier.

Where once the carpenter took great care to give his best to every task, he now found himself satisfied with doing the minimum that was being asked. Over time, his commitment to quality and desire to produce something superior surrendered to shoddy workmanship.

His eye for excellence gradually gave way to accepting a product that was inferior.

It was an unfortunate way to end an otherwise exemplary career.

When the carpenter finished his work and the company's owner came to inspect the house, he walked through quietly, never pointing out the errors or commenting on its sub-standard condition. Instead, he simply handed the front-door key to the carpenter, generously saying: "This is your house, my gift to you...a gift for your many years of faithful service."

Immediately, the carpenter was overcome by a sense of shock and shame. Shock at the immensity of the gift and shame at the realization he had fallen far short of his potential. Had he known he was building his own house, he now realized he would have done it all so differently. Now he had to live in a home he had built none too well.

As may be the case with many of us.

We too are entrusted with great gifts. However, be it in our homes, our workplaces, our worship spaces, or our communities, we too are often tempted to give less than our best. At important points in our lives, we find it is easier to step down instead of step up. Sadly, we all can likely recall moments in which we, like the carpenter, failed to invest the full measure of our skills, talents and abilities to complete a project of our own.

But fortunately, it need not be this way.

Imagine what could be accomplished if each of us chose to see ourselves as carpenters whose every effort is a reflection of our commitment to quality? How might our relationships be enriched, our work environment enhanced, our world improved if everything we did spoke of our desire to create something meant to withstand the test of time?

Be it in hammering a proverbial nail, placing a board, or building a wall, what if our desire to produce something superior with our lives overshadowed any willingness to accept that which is inferior? What if we took great care to give our best to every task, never satisfied with doing just the minimum that was being asked? What if we too approached all we did with the same orientation as the generous company owner, intent to being a blessing to those around us?

*   *   *

To many, the word blessing is something that makes sense to hear at church on Sunday but has no place in the workplace on Monday. It's something we routinely say when someone sneezes, yet fail to appreciate its power to enhance the lives of those around us — our workmates, classmates, teammates, friends, family, and spouses.

Thus, to bless others is less affection, more a decision. It's less a feeling, more an action. To bless others is to spend less time focused on ourselves and more time interested in building value into the lives of those around us. With this perspective in mind, here are five no-fail things that you can begin doing today to **BLESS** others in all you say and do:

> **Be Present:** In our frenzied, fast-paced world, distractions abound. There is no shortage of people or things vying for our time. Unfortunately, many of us quickly lose sight of the fact that our hurried interactions and fractured attention robs us of the joy and satisfaction that comes from allowing ourselves to be fully present in the moment. We would be wise to remember that one of the most profound ways to be a blessing to others is to consciously slow down and be genuinely interested in what the person right in front of you has to say.

> **Listen Deeply:** As a leader, it's difficult to really know what others are thinking, what's troubling them or how to try and help them, unless you take the time to really listen to them. Paying genuine attention to what others have to say is one of your most potent tools to communicate to those around you that they have value. So commit to using your ears more than your mouth. You may be pleasantly surprised at what you hear...and learn.

Encourage Frequently: Courage. Encourage. Two words, same origin; an others-centered attitude. To encourage is to demonstrate by your words and your actions that you care. It affirms to those around you, especially when they are struggling to achieve a goal or to make progress in pursuing a dream, that you are willing to make what is important to them important to you. Choose to infuse enthusiasm and energy into the lives of others by being a frequent encourager and watch them flourish, thrive, and come fully alive.

Serve Selflessly: Some people believe making a significant difference in someone's life demands we do something big or bold that will turn a lot of heads. We tend to think *Extreme Makeover: Home Edition* instead of realizing blessings more frequently come in the form of small, sincere acts of service. Be it picking up an extra shift for a coworker so they can attend a child's school play, volunteering to help a transitioning veteran build a resume, or offering to help your spouse cook a meal, clean the kitchen, or mow the lawn after a long arduous day, don't look past the small, ordinary opportunities right before you to selflessly serve those around you.

Sacrifice Willfully: This is not a word that easily rolls off the tongue, nor is it a concept our society naturally enjoys or embraces. After all, to sacrifice infers giving something up. It speaks to accepting less than we desire or believe we deserve. Yet, leadership in a company, community, or in your family requires sacrifice. It demands you be willing to surrender having your way for the benefit of blessing those who look to you, depend on you, or are able to be influenced by you.

With all this said, here is what I hope you take away. To be a blessing is to make the most of every opportunity you have to be present when you are with others, to take the time to truly listen to others, to encourage and selflessly serve others, and to choose to sacrifice for others. I am not saying it will be easy, but I can tell you that this is necessary if you are intent on being the leader you want to be and whom others deserve to see.

True leadership, the kind that leaves the world better than when you found it, is rooted in a decision to be others-centered instead of self-centered. It's about using the time you have this side of eternity to *bless* others — starting at home, extending to your workplace, and spilling over into your worship space and community.

Remember, this is the only life you will ever build.

Resolve to build it well.

15

Lead for a Higher Purpose

"The purpose of human life is to serve, and to show compassion and the will to help others."
Albert Schweitzer

It has been called the greatest photograph of all time. It may well be the most widely reproduced, even winning the Pulitzer Prize for photography. Snapped on February 23, 1945 as our nation was fighting its way across the Pacific as part of the island hopping campaign in World War II, it served as the symbol for the Seventh War Loan Drive; was used on a postage stamp; appeared on the cover of countless magazines and newspapers across the globe; and even served as the model for the Marine Corps War Memorial that today stands in Arlington, Virginia—a timeless symbol of the cost our military members are willing to bear in defending the values, ideas, and principles this great nation was originally founded upon.

The famous picture of five marines and a navy corpsman struggling to raise the flag atop Mount Suribachi on the tiny island of Iwo Jima in the middle of the Pacific Ocean perfectly captures the sense of momentum of six men straining toward a common goal. In this instance, that goal was to mark claim to the most strategic point on the island following one of the costliest battles in Marine Corps history.

Its toll of 6,821 Americans dead, 5,931 of them Marines, accounted for nearly one-third of all Marine Corps losses in all of World War II.

Eyewitness accounts confirm that the raising of the flag on the fourth day of the bloody battle of Iwo Jima ignited a wave of energy and enthusiasm that could be heard across the island. Just as the battle was bogging down and progress was reduced to mere inches an hour, the moment that red, white, and blue of our nation's flag was seen proudly flying atop that hilltop, American troops were filled with a new found vigor and vitality. The momentum of that moment subsequently inspired them to push through to achieve the mission of conquering what would become the first Japanese homeland soil to be captured by the Americans.

In my view, this inspiring story of these six courageous men reminds us of the true definition of leadership. That is, it's not designed to be a position we earn or seek but rather is meant to be *a responsibility we choose to fulfill*, a choice to step outside our comfort zones and do what we can, when we can, where we can to have more impact, make more of a difference, and lead our lives for a higher purpose.

*   *   *

Whether we realize it or not, we all want to lead our lives for a higher purpose. In fact, science confirms we are wired from birth to contribute to a cause larger than ourselves. Sociologist Ernest Becker writes, "Man will lay down his life for his country, his society, his family. He will choose to throw himself on a grenade to save his comrades; he is capable of the highest generosity and self-sacrifice. But he has to feel and believe that what he is doing is truly heroic, timeless, and supremely meaningful."

What Becker is reminding us of is the fact that achieving true happiness and satisfaction in life requires us to pursue goals that are relevant, honorable, and that contribute to creating the kind of society we each desire and deserve. Life cannot be merely about us. If we want to thrive as citizens and as a nation, we must figure out what each of us can do to roll up our sleeves and do something to add value to our surroundings—one opportunity at a time.

One inspiring leader who is answering the call to do just that is Karen Ross.

Karen is the CEO of the New York-based strategic technology, staffing and project management company *Sharp Decisions*. For almost a quarter of a century, her organization has been providing best in class technology services to both national and international clients. And she's done so by building her business on the same timeless values as those who serve in the United States Armed Forces—namely integrity, professionalism, and dedication.

Upon hearing of many veterans' difficult plight to successfully reintegrate into society, and despite having no formal connection to the military, she decided to get serious about doing something to help these young heroes establish a new, sustainable path forward. Contributing $250,000 of her own money, she began the one-of-a-kind V.E.T.S. (Vocations, Education and Training for ServiceMembers) program.

V.E.T.S is designed to help provide former service members with valuable, in demand technology skills such as software testing and data mining capabilities. Although there are certainly numerous programs across the country designed to help return military veterans to the workforce, this program is unique in that it is grounded in one of the military's most treasured and timeless principles: teamwork.

You see, Karen and her team not only equip veterans with valuable individual technical skills, they actually place these warriors in small teams of three or four people so they can support one another in their journey of developing relevant new life skills. This happens not for a week or a month, mind you, but for as long as it takes to provide these talented young veterans with the confidence and strength to successfully set off on their own.

I would offer, Karen Ross provides us a glimpse into leadership in its most basic, fundamental form. That is, much like those brave young Marines decades ago who selflessly chose to risk raising the American flag on Iwo Jima, her example reminds us that leadership isn't designed to be a position we earn or seek, rather it is meant to be *a responsibility we choose to fulfill,* a choice to step outside our comfort zones and do what we can, when we can, where we can to have more impact, make more of a difference, and lead our lives for a higher purpose.

One opportunity at a time.

16

Refuse to Settle for Good Enough

"Leadership is the capacity and will to rally
men and women to a common purpose, and
the character which inspires confidence."
Lord Montgomery

The history of warfare is replete with examples of how success in complex endeavors hinges on proactive, creative and effective leadership. For instance, the movements of the armies of Napoleon startled the world until an equal in Wellington appeared. In Africa, Rommel was considered to be a brilliant tactician who was virtually unstoppable. That is until Generals Alexander and Montgomery arrived and ended Rommel's battlefield dominance.

What this reveals is leadership is largely about creating something new. It is about promoting innovation, breakthroughs, and discovery, all of which require a disruption of the status quo. While managers are hard at work bringing efficiency and effectiveness to business policies, processes, and products, positive leaders are busy pointing the way to new horizons and guiding others in more empowering directions.

Having designed and directed a sweeping strategy development effort for America's $14 billion agency responsible for worldwide deployment and sustainment of military forces and material, I've also lived the reality of trying to bring positive change to large, bureaucratic organizations. Yet, be it in peace or war, I've discovered making a commitment to never settle for good enough in order to try and bring out the best in those around you demands we keep several important perspectives in mind. Specifically:

Resolve to Craft Your Vision in Pencil, Not Ink: It is a well-accepted role of leaders to focus on the future and pursue the possibility it holds. In other words, leading entails being a visionary. It speaks to confidently looking ahead and ascertaining how to best transform your current reality into a prudent path toward your desired future. Although I certainly won't argue the importance of a leader as visioneer, I will highlight that one of the most significant errors I see leaders consistently make is developing their vision in isolation and then expecting people to accept it at face value. Unfortunately, when leaders do so they violate one of the most important truths associated with promoting change. Namely, *our words create our worlds*. How we choose to describe and discuss what we are doing and where we are going is important, but what moves people to sustainable, self-motivated action is understanding the why behind the vision. This can only be fully realized if leaders involve others in the process of co-creating their desired future state.

> **Action:** Ultimately, what makes a vision come to life isn't that people understand it, but that they choose to own it. Intentionally involve others in determining the most prudent path to take to get from where you are today to where you desire to be tomorrow. Don't direct or demand others follow your vision. Encourage them to help you refine your vision. Making inclusivity a priority increases ownership of a common purpose, enhances motivation, improves information-sharing, and results in leaders making wiser, more informed choices.

**Believe No Job is too Small or Insignificant for Anyone...
Especially You:** For those of us who have served in uniform,
getting dirty, sleeping in tents, leading marches in the mud or
spending hours rehearsing a mission comes with the territory.
As a commander, you don't get a pass because you have the
highest rank. In fact, you should be ready to be the first to
face hardship and the last to benefit from success. If your
team is cold, wet, hungry and sleepless, you should be too.
You should be prepared to eat last, own failure and generously
share triumphs. This *others-centered* approach to leading will
build deep trust and enduring respect and reinforce that you
don't expect anyone on your team to do anything you wouldn't
do yourself.

> **Action:** Ego tempts many leaders to travel the road of
> self-aggrandizement. The higher the position in the
> hierarchy, the greater the rank, the more pronounced the
> pull toward self-promotion. Choose to direct your effort
> and attention toward what you can give rather than what
> you can receive. Demonstrate humility, not superiority.
> Model for others the selfless attitudes and behaviors you
> desire to see in them.

Remember that Leaders should be Generalists not Specialists:
The most effective leaders are generalists who make it a priority
to hire outstanding specialists. Nobody can be an expert
in everything; but the greater your scope of responsibility
as a leader, the more you need to learn about what you are
demanding of your people. Just like the best sports coaches
who invest countless hours understanding every position on
the field, positive leaders develop a keen sense of how the
organization's various roles, functions, systems, people and
processes contribute to achieving the desired goals, objectives
or missions. You may be a specialist at one thing, but knowing

what others do around you (and how and why they are doing it), is vital to not only attaining your desired outcomes, but realizing your full individual and collective potential.

> **Action**: Don't allow yourself to become stale or small-minded. Make it a personal priority to know more about what is going on around you. If you spent the bulk of your career working in sales, accept a stretch assignment in business development or talent management. You will likely be pleasantly surprised at how this broader, richer view of what's happening in your organization will enlarge your perspective, enhance your appreciation, and elevate your sense of personal satisfaction.

Recognize every interaction is an opportunity to leave a trace ... for good or bad: The world of physics has a common principle which dictates, "Every contact leaves a trace." What this illuminates for leaders is the fact that every interaction with someone, be it verbally, in written form, or even via non-verbal mannerisms, makes an impression. Effective leaders understand this and know every engagement with others—a secretary, sales associate, store room clerk, or CEO—is a potentially powerful means of nurturing a relationship, eliminating an obstruction to progress, or reinforcing trust. The greater your rank, higher your position, or more significant your influence, the more profound is your potential effect. So determine to leave a trace that leaves those around you better for knowing you.

> **Action:** Do your part to seed an environment where everyone is compelled by your example to contribute their full potential. Adopt a *Walk the Floor Policy* instead of an Open Door Policy. Visit with people in their space, don't make them come to yours.

The best positive leaders I've known or studied all shared a common trait: They were unwilling to settle for the existing state of affairs. In other words, they never settled for "good enough." They believed with all their hearts that what we focus on can become reality. Where managers are content to accept the old mantra, "If it isn't broken don't fix it," the leaders I admire most are those who believe, "If it isn't broken, break it and start anew … only better."

These elements of leadership are not easy to execute on a consistent basis. They require a daily focus, keen attention, and relentless commitment to leaving your part of the world better than you first found it. So make it a habit to ask yourself, with each move and decision you make, "Am I being the best possible leader I can be right now? If not, what can I do to adjust accordingly?"

It's a habit everyone will be grateful you make a priority. Perhaps no one more so than you.

17

Don't Be Afraid to Toss Out the Rule Book

"Mindless habitual behavior is the enemy of innovation."
Rosabeth Moss Kanter

"Houston, we have a problem!"

These five words, originally spoken over forty years ago by astronaut, Jack Swigert of Apollo 13 on April 14, 1970, immediately captured the attention of citizens the world over.

The warning to the Houston Space Center of a major technical fault in the electrical system of one of the spacecraft's oxygen tanks certainly caused well-founded concern. It also immediately sent technicians and scientists into a full-fledged search for innovative solutions to this unexpected life-threatening situation.

For the next seventy-two hours, scores of people worked around the clock to determine what could be done to bring the astronauts safely home. Creativity meters soared, innovative ideas were explored, and no possible remedy was ignored. And, as lead flight director of Mission Control, Gene Kranz, made abundantly clear to everyone involved, although failure was a possibility, it "just wasn't an option."

The ensuing effort was far more than a contest of athletic, technological, or engineering prowess. This was something different. It was more of a high-stakes drama of solution-finding played out with limited resources against unknown odds. It was also a moment in which the only real hope of turning things around demanded that everyone involved jettison their old ways of thinking. The well-rehearsed routines, the existing "book answers", and the standard "way we've always done things" weren't going to be sufficient to save Apollo 13.

With the realization that rote answers would no longer suffice, something magical happened. Everyone involved found themselves liberated to dig deep within their imaginations to find a creative means to shape a desirable end. The entrepreneurial spirit of the amazingly innovative and empowering effort that ensued set off a chain reaction that elevated personal performance. All of which was brilliantly exemplified in Kranz's charge to the team to "...forget the flight plan. From this moment on, we are improvising a new mission. How do we get our men home?"

And home they did get them.

On 17 April, 1970, three days after that now famous call for assistance, millions across the globe watched as Apollo 13 and its crew splashed down safely into the Indian Ocean. Their rescue providing the world with one of the most powerful demonstrations of solution-finding ever recorded. A reminder of how we often experience our highest creativity when there is the most at stake and failure is a possibility but not an option.

* * *

Stories like Apollo 13 encourage and inspire us by reflecting humanity at its best. They remind us effective innovation is rarely a function of stringently pursuing a particular ideal but rather, it is a byproduct of remaining open to the art of the possible. Although idealists and dreamers stubbornly go down with the ship, innovators have the foresight to grab the rudder and change course. As Amazon.com founder, Jeff Bezos, likes to point out, "People who are right a lot of the time are the same people who change their minds a lot of the time," especially when the facts prove them wrong or their circumstances demand setting off in different direction.

Here's the good news. You don't have to be an astronaut, engineer, serial entrepreneur, or find yourself smack in the middle of a crisis to initiate the innovation process. You just have to believe there is a better way. Perhaps best of all, you don't even have to be the one who comes up with the better way. You just have to recognize that your greatest seemingly insurmountable challenges often contain the seeds of your most significant innovations.

With this in mind, here are several lessons from the events of Apollo 13 that we can apply in our own surroundings to become the kind of innovative leaders we want to be and others deserve to see.

Leverage a Crisis to Promote Out-of-the-Box Thinking: The instant the moon no longer became the goal, everything the team faced, both in space and on the ground, posed a new challenge and presented a new opportunity. It forced people to set aside their entrenched opinions and ideas. It demanded they reevaluate their options and question everything they were doing. At the same time, it forced them to redefine success. It was only when business as usual was ruled out that real progress toward a viable solution commenced.

Don't be Too Quick to Cut and Run: When things don't go according to plan, the automatic reflex is to find ways to bail out rather than stay put and try to turn things around for the better. This intuitive response is understandable given that change is hard. Unfortunately, life has a way of teaching us if we cut and run too early, we will almost certainly miss the opportunity to bring our greatest creativity to bear on a situation. Think about it. From the moment everyone associated with Apollo 13 recognized thinking differently about both the problem and the solution was to bring the astronauts safely home, everything became a possibility. Once "out of bound" options and previously untenable alternatives suddenly become permissible solutions, innovation flourished and success was transformed from a desirable possibility into a tangible reality.

Refuse to Blindly Guard the Past: The only way a leader and the team can overcome their natural tendency to protect the past at the cost of the future is to find ways to identify and release the gifted innovators in their midst. For example, once the flight director of Mission Control encouraged those around him to toss out the rule book, people figured out ways to transfer energy from the coffee maker to help power the self-contained lunar module, which itself was transformed into the main duty cabin. Round holes were transformed to accommodate square plugs to keep the carbon-monoxide buffers working, and power from non-critical instruments and systems was rerouted so it could be stored for the spacecraft to reenter earth's atmosphere. All of this proved essential to the safe return of three brave American astronauts to earth seventy-two hours after hearing that memorable phrase, "Houston, we have a problem."

Believe Adversity Creates Opportunity to Unleash the Best in Anyone: As the events of Apollo 13 confirm, unexpected circumstances create unprecedented opportunity for anyone and everyone to elevate their game and demonstrate their value. Once people quit primarily looking to those with formal titles, specific positions, and particular roles for a remedy, ingenuity increased, creativity skyrocketed, and nothing was deemed outside consideration as a possible option. And as a result, the seemingly impossible became possible--Proof positive how our greatest insurmountable problems often contain the seeds of our most significant innovations.

What I hope you take away from this story is that none of the positive effects of the people's actions were realized by fearing change.

Instead, each of them was the result of leveraging an opportunity for individuals to risk stepping out of their comfort zones to make different, more empowering choices. It's a lesson we should all remember the next time we find ourselves in a situation where much is at stake and failure is a possibility, but not an option.

18

Put the "T" Back in Self-Control

*"Self-reverence, self-knowledge, self-control; these
three alone lead one to sovereign power."*
Alfred Lord Tennyson

Growing up, my childhood baseball hero was Pete Rose. In addition to his amazing ability to consistently hit solid base hits, I was particularly mesmerized by his all-out style of play. No matter what he was doing, swinging the bat, guarding the plate, or stealing a base, Pete Rose played to win. He gave 100 percent of his effort to every game, wowed millions of adoring fans along the way, and earned the nickname, "Charlie Hustle."

Then, just like that, everything changed.

When the story broke that Rose committed the unpardonable sin in baseball—betting on games his team played—the sports world was stunned. Rose, who was on track to be the all-time hit king, suddenly left fans questioning his motives and distrusting his intentions. In the blink of an eye, my hero became a zero.

In his autobiography called *My Prison Without Walls*, Rose shares, "I was aware of my records and my place in baseball history. But I was never aware of boundaries or able to control that part of my life. Admitting that I was out of control has been next to impossible for me...how could I be so disciplined in one part of my life—and so reckless in another?"

I have to admit the very public fall of one-time superstar Pete Rose still saddens me. After all, no one wants to see someone so talented fall from grace. But for all the disappointment associated with this unfortunate truth, a very important lesson emerges we would all be wise to heed. Namely, it can be hard to exercise self-control in an out-of-control world.

Admittedly, self-control, otherwise known as temperance, is not popular in today's culture. I would offer it has become counter-cultural. In fact, much of our society appears to prefer pursuing self-gratification over exercising self-discipline. It's never been easier to become so self-absorbed that we lose sight of what really matters.

It is virtually impossible today to pick up any magazine or newspaper, turn on any television, or tune into any radio station without someone trying to convince us we should strive for more. We are awash in a culture where it is easy to succumb to the never ending barrage of slick advertising campaigns and compelling commercials that seek to persuade us to never truly be satisfied with who we are, what we have or what we are doing. In this kind of culture, practicing temperance, *the ability to look outside ourselves in a way that balances a healthy self-denial with a deep seated commitment to live up to a particular standard*, isn't easy.

But I'm here to tell you it is very necessary.

Be it as simple as staying true to a diet, refusing to succumb to peer pressure or refraining from lashing out at someone who has hurt us deeply, temperance prevents us from going down the same path as one time baseball great Pete Rose and caving into irrationality and poor judgment.

This is an important point to discern. After all, as leaders in our homes, workplaces, worship spaces, and communities, we want to make a difference. We want our leadership to be felt. And that's okay. However, challenges arise when pressures to perform lead us to make decisions that are more about ourselves than they are about the best interests of our organizations; our families; our customers; or our constituents. When we allow our undisciplined egos, unchecked ambitions or unrealistic expectations to get the better of us, watch out. We've set ourselves on a path that all but guarantees we will fall far short of our potential.

Several years ago, management gurus Jim Collins and Morten T. Hansen set out to study how successful leaders routinely positioned themselves and their companies for success in turbulent times. They looked at more than twenty thousand companies and poured over countless reams of data to ascertain why some organizations thrived in uncertainty and others did not. At the end of their exhaustive analysis, they concluded, "[Successful leaders] are not more creative. They're not more visionary. They're not more charismatic. They're not more ambitious. They're not more heroic. And they're not more prone to making big, bold moves."

So what was it they discovered that truly set great leaders apart from the rest?

It came down to one primary characteristic. Temperance. Namely, "They all led their teams with a surprising method of self-control in an out-of-control world." In other words, the most effective leaders made self-discipline a priority, not an afterthought.

Ask yourself, "What areas in my life require more self-discipline?" Challenge yourself to identify several areas where temperance is not your strong suit. It could be in your diet, your relationships, your exercise routine, how you spend your leisure time, or how you treat your spouse, children or coworkers. If you want to be the leader you are capable of being, resolve today to take tangible steps to build greater self-control into your life.

Remember, practicing temperance is choosing to make a decision today to live better than you did yesterday. It's developing discipline from the inside out. It's making the commitment to practice self-control in life's everyday moments so you don't find yourself one day making reckless bets that undermine your example, dilute your effectiveness and destroy your legacy.

As the sad story of one-time baseball icon and childhood hero Pete Rose affirms, without temperance, you'll eventually stop liking who you are. Don't gamble with your influence. Commit to becoming a person worth following.

19

Seek a More Excellent Way

"We are all born originals - why is it
so many of us die copies?"
Edward Young

Different is good.

In fact, I believe different can be very, very good.

Of course, thinking and being different than those around you is easier said than done. After all, going against the flow, thinking outside the box, or deviating from what everyone else is doing is almost certainly uncomfortable if not outright unsettling.

But what if I were to tell you being different is exactly what's needed to flourish and thrive in today's dynamic, fast-paced, ever-changing world? At a time in our nation's history when we need more people to step up to help make a positive difference in our homes, workplaces, worship spaces, and communities, it seems many of us are content to merely settle—more intent to stick with the perceived safety of the status quo than to risk taking a stand for what we truly believe is worth fighting for in our lives.

And it's a big mistake.

You see, everywhere we look today the status quo is hard at work convincing us it's better to stay put and keep doing more of the same. Be it doing the same unrewarding job, sticking with the same unhealthy relationship or promoting the same dysfunctional politics, the status quo strives to keep us narrowly and selfishly focused. Divided instead of united, it compels us to work on individual agendas instead of toward collective solutions to persistent personal, professional, or societal problems.

In our own lives, allowing the status quo to have its way with us serves as a barrier to forward motion. It creates individual, organizational, and relational obstacles that keep us from becoming the best version of ourselves. Be it a destructive habit, a persistent problem, or an undeveloped skill, the status quo strives to keep us squarely in our comfort zones and subtly persuades us *to accept mediocrity as the norm.*

Lulling us into adopting what I term *a mediocre me mindset.*

A Mediocre Me Mindset

The dictionary aptly defines mediocrity as "*moderate to inferior in quality.*" Derived from the French term of the same spelling, mediocre literally means "halfway up the mountain," insinuating how accepting mediocrity is to fail to achieve one's objective or fall short of attaining one's potential.

In our own lives, accepting mediocrity as the norm prevents us from becoming the best possible version of ourselves. It strives to keep us squarely in our comfort zones and subtly persuades us to settle for so much less than we are capable of achieving. For example, despite our knowing there is a different way or a different plan that could help us move in the direction of our dreams, aspirations, and objectives, mediocrity convinces us to disengage and do or say nothing. And why shouldn't we? After all, going along with the herd instead of doing something to break from established convention is certainly safe.

Now please don't get me wrong. We have all undoubtedly found ourselves in that awkwardly comfortable position of settling at one time or another on this journey we call life. But the real problem occurs when settling becomes the norm. Like a good habit gone bad;

an addiction gone wild, the price of routinely settling for mediocrity and refusing to bring our best selves to whatever it is we are doing costs all of us dearly.

But the good news is it doesn't have to remain this way.

I believe every one of us, regardless of where we find ourselves in the proverbial hierarchy, social order, or organizational chart, can expand our view of the potential role we can play in the world. "How?" you ask. Simply by beginning to exert a very powerful form of others-centered leadership.

What I mean is, instead of thinking about leadership in narrow terms, such as believing we must possess a particular title, rank, or role before we can initiate the change we want to see occur in our surroundings, we opt to view leadership as *a choice*. Specifically, a choice to live out the belief that there is no problem or challenge too big to tackle, no solution too elusive for us to discover when we are sold-out to adding value to the world around us.

Sound too farfetched, idealistic or straightforward to be true?

I certainly don't think so. Let me share with you the three choices consistently emulated by the world's most effective positive change leaders. And the best part is, none of these choices demand we pursue further training, acquire specific titles, or develop special skills in order to get started transforming the raw material of our lives into something that will leave our part of the world better than we first found it:

> **Develop New Eyes to See:** I recently read about a man in Maine who, for one morning every month, pretends to be blind. He wakes without opening his eyes, fumbles his way to his kitchen to make coffee then heads off to the bathroom to shower and brush his teeth. He eats a bowl of cold cereal and dresses himself and doesn't open his eyes until he gets behind the wheel of his car to go to work. He does this so he can appreciate the many gifts in his life, among them the gift of sight.

In today's world, it is easy to become entitled, losing sight of the things that really matter. Don't let that be you. Resolve to build habits in your life that will help you remain grateful for all you possess. It will make you a happier, healthier, more successful person inside and out.

Never give up on People: All of us walk through the world with our own baggage. We begin acquiring these burdens as children and they accumulate as we travel through life. The challenge that arises, however, is that over time we begin to get so weighed down by our past experiences that it impacts how we deal with our present circumstances, leading us to be less patient, trustful and accommodating than we should be with others.

We should never forget that life is first and foremost about relationships. None of us were created to proceed through our journey alone. But when we begin to allow our past hurts, disappointments, fears or failures to influence how we interact with the people around us, we begin replacing love, patience and kindness with jealousy, possessiveness, and suspicion, leading us to live lives far smaller and narrower than we are capable of living.

The fact of the matter is, people are sometimes going to let you down. This is a fact of life. It is our responsibility to not give up on people but, rather, to commit to doing what we can to always believe the best and strive to bring out the best in them. Trust me. It will make a profoundly positive difference in the quality of your life and the quality of your relationships.

Strive to be of Service: Serving others is the highest form of human expression and has long been known to be the key to true physical, mental, emotional and spiritual health and happiness. Yet we must keep in mind that it isn't an act of kindness if you expect something in return. Once you remove the payoff from the equation, you will find yourself catapulted to the next level of true selflessness, understanding that the reward for loving is love; the reward for serving others is being of service; the reward for leading well is doing your part to leave the world better than you first found it.

The self-esteem that comes from reaching out and helping other people is invaluable. It gets us out of our own heads and helps us not feel overwhelmed by problems or other concerns. It helps us feel connected and represents the essence of what it means to lead a life of true purpose, meaning and significance. Why should you consider taking this advice to heart? Because surveys confirm that the desire to achieve something meaningful and significant in and through our lives is important. In fact, reams of research affirms that millions of us—more than three out of every four adults—say we are interested in making a positive difference in the world. We want to become the best version of ourselves and have our lives characterized by such terms as relevant, significant, and, dare I say, *excellent.*

Of course, none of these things will occur by accident. We have to choose to transform ordinary moments in life into opportunities to build value into our surroundings. After all, we cannot expect to build a successful organization, or enjoy mutually beneficial relationships, or achieve anything of real value if we aren't willing to replace a mediocre me mindset with a resolute commitment to making the most of our moment by moment opportunities to courageously influence, guide, inspire, and shape the course of events in our sphere of influence.

The late American author and poet Maya Angelou once taught that courage is the most important of all the virtues because, without it, you cannot practice any of the others consistently. It takes courage to be true to yourself; just as it takes courage to develop new eyes to see; to never give up on people; to strive to be of service; to focus on the present rather than be paralyzed by the past; to genuinely and lovingly accept others; and to be content with who we are today while striving to grow closer to our potential tomorrow. It takes courage to be different from the crowd and commit to leading our lives in a more excellent way.

Remember, change always begins in our mind. The way we choose to think determines the way we feel and the way we feel influences the way we act. If we allow ourselves to be filled with fear of the future, we can't change much, and the status quo will continue to have its way with us. But if we are open to going against the flow, thinking outside the box, or deviating from what everyone else is doing in order to prompt positive change in our surroundings, there is no limit to what we can do—prompting each and every one of us to recognize we are already as much of a leader as we *choose* to be.

20

Unleash Your Entrepreneurial Edge

"Decide that you want it more than you are afraid of it."
Bill Cosby

It's unlikely Wolfgang Kohler had any reason to believe that when he conducted his now famous monkey experiments on Canary Island in the early 1900s he was providing us, almost a century later, with a powerful symbol of what it takes to win in today's world.

Kohler, a psychologist, arranged an experimental cage in which he placed several different sized boxes and other objects. He then hung a plump bushel of bananas high in the cage so they would be inaccessible to the monkeys. After releasing the monkeys into the cage, it didn't take them long to notice their favorite delicacy positioned high above their heads. Most of the monkeys proceeded to jump around, whooping and hollering. Although all the monkeys had their gazes firmly fixed on the bananas, none of them even came close to possessing them.

But it turns out one pair of monkeys was different from the others.

Instead of swinging from the side of the cage and jumping for the bananas without any real chance of achieving success, these two sat and quietly absorbed all that was arrayed around them. Then they made their bold move.

While all the other monkeys were busy doing the same old thing, the two thoughtful monkeys began collecting the boxes that were strewn across the cage. After dragging them to the middle, they then rearranged them one on top of the other. And just like that, this pair of innovative primate engineers were able to easily reach the bushel of delicious bananas—much to the delight of their less creative monkey friends.

*   *   *

Some of you may be wondering what lesson we can derive from this unusual tale. From a very early age, we are conditioned to believe it's okay to go along if it will help us get along, and frequently, this works for us. Unfortunately, most of us never break out of this type of thinking and, as a result, we become like the majority of monkeys in the story whose inability to deviate from the status quo left them hungrily staring at a delicious prize that was seemingly too far out of reach.

What I find particularly noteworthy about this story is that, as is often the case, the solution to the problem (in this case, building a ladder out of the boxes), was right before the monkeys' eyes the entire time. Everything needed to turn a delicious dream into a practical reality (and a full belly) was already present. It only took two monkeys out of the whole group to choose to look beyond their circumstances. Only they saw the boxes not only for what they were, but also for what they could be.

How often do we find ourselves doing the same thing?

Scientists specializing in how our brains function tell us it's typical for us to address challenges we encounter with a reproductive mindset, meaning, when confronted with a problem or unfamiliar situation, we fixate on finding something in our past that has worked for us. We ask ourselves, "What have I been taught in life, education, or work to solve the problem?" Then we analytically select the most promising approach based on previous experiences.

In contrast, the most successful leaders think productively, not reproductively. When they come across an unfamiliar situation or a problem, they ask themselves questions such as, "How many different ways can I look at this?" "How can I rethink the way I see my current circumstances?" or "How many different ways can I devise to solve this new or novel challenge?" In effect, productive thinkers strive to generate as many alternative approaches as they can.

Albert Einstein was once asked what the difference was between him and the average person. He said that if you asked the average person to find a needle in a haystack, the person would stop when he or she found a needle. He, on the other hand, would tear through the entire haystack looking for all the possible needles.

Here's my point. The only way you can ever expect to be more and do more with your life is to understand that, sometimes, you have to be willing to go above and beyond what others are doing around you. In order to creatively solve problems and capitalize on new opportunities, you must be willing to abandon the desire to rely on past experience and reconceptualize the situation. In other words, you must be willing to think productively. Pursuing the path of least resistance just because that's what everyone else is doing just won't bring home the bananas.

As George Bernard Shaw so aptly reminds us, "The people who get on in this world are the people who get up and look for the circumstances they want, and if they can't find them, make them." Be that person. Don't be afraid to unleash your entrepreneurial spirit on the world. Choose to live life by your rules, not someone else's.

So remember this. If you want to take your organization to the next level, look for those in your ranks who are willing to think differently, act boldly and be and do more. Find the innovative 'monkeys' in your midst and promote them while passing the closed-minded 'monkeys' to your competitors ... and watch who ends up with the bigger stack of bananas at the end of the day.

21

Avoid the Trenches

"An army of a thousand is easy to find, but,
ah, how difficult to find a good general."
Chinese Proverb

In 1904, France and Britain signed the Entente Cordiale (the friendly understanding); shortly thereafter, Russia also agreed to join this alliance. As a result, the German military began to fear the possibility of a combined attack from France, Britain and Russia.

In an attempt to respond to what they perceived as a growing threat, the German staff began making plans of their own to fend off a potential attack from these allied powers. The plan became known as The Von Schlieffen Plan, named after its primary architect, German Army Chief of Staff Alfred von Schlieffen.

In 1906 the plan was modified so that the main route of German counter attack would now be through the flat plains of Flanders, Belgium. The assumption was that Belgium's small army would be unable to stop German forces from quickly entering France. This, in turn, would enable Germany to defeat France before Russia was ready to mobilize and employ all of its forces.

Or so they thought.

In 1914, the spark that lit the fuse for the First World War occurred when Austrian Archduke Francis Ferdinand (heir to the

Austro-Hungarian throne) and his wife Sophia were assassinated while riding in the motorcade through the streets of Sarajevo. The situation quickly escalated and, by August of that year, all of the major European powers via their complex series of alliances were pulled into the Great War. It also set the stage for Germany to put into motion The Von Schlieffen Plan.

Things, however, didn't quite work out as the Germans had planned. Instead of advancing quickly, they were held up by tenacious Belgian forces and surprised by how quickly the British Army was able to reinforce both France and Belgium. Ultimately, the Germans were stopped in France before they could reach their final destination of Paris. The war quickly became a stalemate, with both sides digging in to create a terrifying new phrase in our vocabulary: "trench warfare."

*   *   *

Most of us are familiar with the concept of trench warfare.

After all, who has not seen the pictures or read the stories of men clamoring out of the long lines of muddy trenches that were so common in World War I? Most of us have likely heard about the millions of men forced to assault an enemy on the other side of a space littered with barbed wire, fallen trees and, often, broken bodies.

Those of us who serve in the military think of the worst when we hear the term trench warfare. It's a word that evokes images of wanton death amidst the most horrific of conditions. It conjures up thoughts of a time when the assumed path to victory seemed to discount the innate value of human life. And perhaps above all, it's a powerful example of the tragedy wrought by choosing the safety of playing defense instead of pressing in and seeking every opportunity to be on offense.

You may be asking yourself what trench warfare has to do with leadership. I'd suggest quite a bit. In fact, I believe it serves as a powerful metaphor for the reality that, if you're leading, then you too are going to experience moments where you feel stuck. Progress is painfully slow. You are entrenched: Standing still when you'd rather be moving forward.

The choice you have to make in these moments seems straightforward. Risk moving out into unknown and potentially hostile territory, or stick with the safety of the trench you are in? Please know that accepting the latter is natural. It is easy. It is, after all, the path of least resistance. But be clear. Settling for the safety of the trench rather than resolving to keep moving forward will come at a very high price in terms of time lost, energy dissipated, resources wasted, and potential squandered.

On the other hand, you can muster the courage to press forward when it would be easier to fall back. You can seek out opportunities to make the most of every situation to move closer to achieving your objective. How to motivate yourself to be more proactive, you ask? Try:

> **Pausing and Thinking**. The process of slowing down to think through the reality of your current situation provides you with a clearer grasp of what you are facing—good, bad and indifferent. It improves your discernment, allowing you to be more intentional in the actions you take and those you don't. And perhaps above all, taking time to calibrate to your surroundings seeds a confidence that subsequently opens the door for spontaneity and creativity.

> **Remember Courage is Organic**. When you seek to pursue and maintain high standards that showcase your talents you learn to discriminate and refine what you do, how you do it and, most importantly, why you are doing it. Once you've garnered this clarity, it will be easier to muster the strength to proactively fight for those values, goals and objectives worth fighting defending.

> **Be Bold in Your Thinking and Being**. Combining disciplined thought with disciplined action serves as an accelerator for your

success. It also instills confidence in those around you. After all, it's a well-established fact that courage begets courage. As such, your followers are more likely to make their own tough decisions and to take responsibility for those decisions when you model the way of thinking and acting you would like to see displayed around you.

Motivate from Within. Motivating yourself to initiate a change or take on a difficult task certainly isn't easy. Yet we all intuitively understand nothing worth fighting for ever is. The key to success is to understand that progress is rarely a byproduct of a single event. Rather, it is an accumulation of small steps that eventually lead to big feats. This simple recognition helps you to keep stepping up and out when conditions make it more appealing to play it safe.

Anyone can choose to play defense in the trenches instead of remaining on offense in the open field. A leader worth following, however, will equip, encourage, empower and ideally inspire you to do all you reasonably can to keep moving forward. As an ancient Chinese proverb wisely reminds us, "He who hesitates before each step spends his life on one leg."

Keep in mind that those committed to doing something to improve conditions around them stand still only long enough to discern the next smart step. Begging the question, how long have you been in the same spot?

Is it possible you have settled for the safety of the trenches?

22

Broaden Your Perspective

"A little perspective, like a little humor, goes a long way."
Allen Klein

July 1863 found our nation embroiled in a costly civil war. That summer, Confederate General Robert E. Lee had led his army north into southern Pennsylvania, hoping to build on the Southern Army's rapidly growing momentum. For three long days, the armies of the North and South were locked in a fierce battle at the small college town of Gettysburg. It was a battle that would result in 50,000 American casualties.

It was also the battle that proved to be the turning point of the war.

As hostilities on the battlefield progressed, both armies sought to capitalize on opportunities to tip the outcome in their favor. Every inch of ground was precious, and both sides knew a single misstep by the other could signal the difference between victory and defeat.

Every advantage was sought.

Every mistake was exploited.

In the midst of the battle, Brigadier General G. K. Warren, Chief Topographical Engineer of the Union Army, climbed to the top of one of two rocky hills to the south of Gettysburg—a hill known to locals as Little Round Top. This site, defended by a small band of his unit's signalmen, held a commanding view of the entire battlefield. From this high ground, the general knew he could observe troop movements, check the placement of key artillery and, perhaps most importantly, relay critical information to his field commanders engaged in combat.

Warren's ascent to the top was not an easy one as his main fighting force was currently engaged in a fierce gun battle with Confederate soldiers. His brigade had already suffered tremendous losses earlier in day. But he knew it was critical he check on his men perched atop the hill.

As the general ascended the final crest, he saw something that made his heart skip a beat. Looking at the forces arrayed below him, it was immediately obvious his Union army had become inadvertently stretched across the battlefield and one of its flanks was severely exposed and extremely vulnerable. Now, instantly able to see for miles, the general could see how the battle would very likely unfold if something didn't change, and change quickly.

Quite unexpectedly, Little Round Top had suddenly become a strategic position that, if lost, could spell disaster for the entire Union army. Now armed with a broader perspective, General Warren also understood how the situation presented an extraordinary opportunity. If his forces succeeded in holding this hill, they could not only prevent the Confederates from placing their artillery upon it, but they could also direct their own efforts in a much more effective, coordinated manner.

Warren requested additional forces and within minutes, one of the general's own brigades arrived to reinforce the position. Some time later, other brigades arrived and together, they successfully defended this key hilltop in what became the pivotal engagement of not only Gettysburg, but likely the entire American Civil War — altering the course of our nation's future and quite possibly, world history, in the process.

*   *   *

As the story of Brigadier General Warren so vividly reminds us, the ability to garner a broader perspective of our situation can prove to be a game changer.

So much of our day as leaders is caught up in dealing with the here and now. Too many meetings, too much information, caught in the middle between satisfying the demands of those we report to at the top and providing guidance to those who depend on us for direction. At a time in human history where technology has enabled us to be engaged in countless conversations simultaneously, it's never been easier to constantly be pulled down into the details and miss the larger understanding of what is actually unfolding around us.

Given the host of competing demands we have for our attention, the only we can we continually determine the best way forward is to make it a regular priority to assess if and how our present actions are *actually* moving us closer to achieving our future objectives. What can you do to help yourself adopt a broader perspective? Here is a starter list.

> **Make Some Quiet Time:** Leadership is both active and reflective. One has to alternate between participating and observing. Walt Whitman described it as being "both in and out of the game." With all of the events and chaos going on in your day, it's often hard to see the big picture. So guard some time every day for thought and reflection. You might be surprised at what you discover.

> **Decide What to Say No to:** Learn to distinguish between what you will say yes to and no to. Often, what pulls us off the desired path is that we lose some of our focus and become overcommitted to pursing the wrong goals, addressing the wrong issues, or are distracted by the wrong priorities. Become clear on what is worthy of your yes and be bold about what you have to say no to. Don't allow yourself to lose sight of your true objective.

Ask Others Their Opinion: The higher up you are in an organization, the more challenging it can be to receive truly candid advice. Seek out no more than half a dozen people who you can trust to look you in the eye and offer their candid, well-intentioned perspective, judgment, and knowledge. Why confine your options to your own limited view? Guard yourself from hearing and seeing only what is comfortable or convenient.

Remember, our perspective as leaders is based on the sum of our knowledge, experiences, and choices. It represents the way we see ourselves and situations, how we judge the relative importance of things occurring around us, and, ultimately, influences our decisions and actions. Don't allow the natural fog and friction of your present circumstances to obscure your view of what is really happening around you. Make it a priority to pause from time to time and gain some perspective. Step away from the all-absorbing details in front of you, and reconnect to the bigger picture unfolding around you. You just might be surprised at what you discover when you make it a priority to routinely take a broader view of your current situation.

23

Grant the Gift of Mulligans

"The weak can never forgive. Forgiveness
is the attitude of the strong."
Mahatma Gandhi

Ask anyone who's remotely familiar with the game of golf who they believe are the most familiar names in the sport. You'd likely hear such legends as Hogan, Nicklaus, Palmer or Woods. All great choices ... all clearly world class golfers.

But let me suggest the name Mulligan. After all, it's a name invoked daily by scores of golfers across the globe.

Admittedly, there is considerable debate about the origins of the term 'mulligan'. However, the most widely accepted focuses on a gentleman named David Mulligan who was a regular at the St. Lambert Country Club in Montreal, Canada, during the 1920s. Mr. Mulligan was a well-to-do hotelier in the first half of the century, a part-owner and manager of the upscale Biltmore Hotel in New York City, as well as several large Canadian hotels.

One story about the origin of the term mulligan recounts it was the result of impulse. One day Mulligan hit a very long drive off the first tee. The problem was the drive went long ... in the wrong direction. So, without seeming to think twice about it, he re-teed and hit again (legend has it his second drive flew straight and true).

His partners found the episode amusing, and decided they'd call this 'gift' a 'mulligan'.

Another story places Mulligan as scheduled to play golf with a group of business associates at St. Lambert Country Club in his hometown of Montreal. On the morning of the outing he drove to pick up his golfing party. The road into the club was reportedly extremely bumpy. To make things even more turbulent, the wind was howling and overall weather conditions were poor. Mulligan was said to be very jumpy and shaking from the difficult drive, so his golf partners graciously extended him the opportunity to forget his initial tee shot (which had found its way into a nearby pond) and begin anew, if he so desired. History does not record if he took them up on their gracious offer.

The final story relates to a day when David Mulligan showed up late to the course. Having scrambled to get out of bed and dressed, he raced to meet his golfing party on time. Apparently he was so frazzled on the first tee that he hit a poor drive. Looking sheepishly at his partners, they agreed to allow Mulligan the opportunity to try to do better by allowing him another tee shot.

Regardless which of these three Mulligan legends is true, they all provide simple, but significant lessons we can apply to our own lives. Namely, they illustrate that a Mulligan is a gift, a chance to begin anew, an opportunity to try to do better in the future after making an error. Described another way, a 'Mulligan' is golf's version of *generous forgiveness*.

*   *   *

For those of us who play golf, a mulligan is granted to a fellow golfer following an errant shot. In life, a mulligan is an act of the will in which we deal graciously with others when we aren't required, or expected, to do so. In other words, it's a choice to forgive that extends beyond words into deeds — undeserved favor we choose to freely give away.

Forgiveness is something virtually all Americans think is good—94% surveyed in a nationwide Gallup poll said it was important to forgive. But sadly, it's not something we frequently choose to offer (in the same survey, only 48% said they usually tried to forgive others).

In the original Greek, the word for forgive literally means 'to release or let go of'. In simple terms then, forgiveness is to willingly surrender your desire to retaliate against the person who hurt you. From such a perspective, extending forgiveness to another is akin to saying, "What the person did to me was wrong. They have hurt me deeply and deserve in some way to pay for their offense. But instead of focusing on retribution, I am choosing to grant them an unwarranted favor. I am making the others-centered choice to generously offer the gift of forgiveness, thus releasing the other from the obligation they have to repay me for their wrongful actions."

Each time we witness an act of forgiveness, we are shown its power to heal or to break a seemingly unending cycle of pain. However, medical and psychological studies repeatedly show that forgiveness is not only good for your soul, but good for your body as well. As it turns out, people who opt to practice forgiveness:

- Benefit from better immune functioning and have lower blood pressure;
- Have better mental health than people who don't forgive;
- Have lower amounts of anger and fewer symptoms of anxiety and depression;
- Maintain more satisfying and longer lasting relationships.

The truth is, when we allow ourselves to feel like a victim or sit around dreaming up how we might retaliate against someone who hurt us, our negative thoughts take a toll on our minds and bodies and, ultimately, on the quality of our lives. On the other hand, when we choose to exercise a 'Mulligan Mentality', we set into motion a powerful cycle of healing that benefits everyone involved.

How generous are you in granting mulligans? Is there a situation or a person you know who could benefit from your undeserved favor today? If the answer is yes, why not make the effort to reach out to them today in a new way. I am certain it may well be one of the healthiest decisions you will ever make.

24

Help Hope Become a Habit

"Everything that is done in the world is done by hope."
Martin Luther

Imagine a tuxedo-clad butler coming toward you where you are seated at a large, elegant table decorated with priceless crystal and beautiful china. He sets before you a silver tray, its gleaming cover as reflective as a mirror. "A gift to you from the master of the house," he states with a crisp English accent.

Immediately you begin to ask yourself, "What waits under the cover?" Is it some delicacy or culinary delight? Or could it be something else ... something even more precious, such as a rare piece of jewelry or perhaps a priceless artifact?

You raise the cover gingerly, heart quickening with anticipation.

The only thing to greet your eyes, however, is the bottom of the silver tray. Empty space in which all you can see is the reflection of your own face.

You cast a disappointed glance at the butler.

"Air," he explains smartly, "rich with oxygen."

Such a gift, of course, elicits little thankfulness under normal circumstances. But how different would things be if that same offering were made to sailors trapped beneath the waves, or a skier buried by an avalanche?

Then, suddenly, it would be viewed as a gift beyond value, making even the most precious of diamonds and rubies worthless trinkets in comparison.

Something so ordinary;

Something so plentiful;

Something we routinely take for granted whose sudden absence may well make the difference between life and death.

Such is the paradoxical nature of the world in which we live. For whether or not we notice, most everyone around us at one time or another has borne the slight bluish tint of anoxia, a shortage of air. Perhaps not literally, mind you, but certainly figuratively. It turns out there is something else, equally as precious as oxygen, of which many of us at one time or another are starved. It is hope—the expectation of future good, without which no human soul can flourish and thrive.

*   *   *

Proverbs 13:12 tells us, "Hope deferred makes the heart sick," and no matter where we find ourselves, be it on the battlefield, in the boardroom, or at the bedside of an ailing loved one, no words in the English language are more devastating to us than hearing, "There is no hope."

Log on to your computer or turn on your radio or TV and you're sure to hear why so many believe that hope is lost. Stories of massive job losses, widespread economic instability, natural disasters, escalating crime, political unrest, terrorist attacks, and military conflict abound.

Even closer to home you may face your own hopelessness—a wayward child; a close friend's failing health; a family member's struggle with addiction; bills that outnumber bank account balances; or, perhaps, the lingering sting of a fractured marriage.

The list of reasons why so many are quick to abandon hope goes on and on.

Yet, amidst this bitter reality, the truth remains that, in the deepest recesses of our souls we all still yearn for hope. More importantly, we need hope. Even in the most troubling of times, something deep within us longs to believe that positive outcomes are still possible, no matter how improbable. At our core we long to believe that things can be better.

After all, it's hope that gives us the strength to stand tall after we've taken a fall;

It's hope that enables us to trust when we are told waiting is a must;

It's hope that allows us to endure when circumstances around us seem so very unsure.

And it's hope that allows us to cling to the expectation of a future good, even when the challenges before us loom incredibly large.

Yes, hope isn't optional. It's necessary. We need hope in our lives. For hope is to the soul what oxygen is to our bodies. Without oxygen, our mind and muscles cease functioning, our blood quits flowing and, within minutes, our physical bodies die.

Similarly, without hope in our lives, depression and despair quickly crowd out peace and joy and, in time, the weight of our hurts, fears, sickness and sadness leaves our hearts broken and our souls empty ... starved for hope.

It's been said that a person can live forty days without food, even four days without water, and four minutes without air, but only four seconds without hope. Hope provides the power to keep us going during our most difficult times. Hope, the expectation of future good, is the fuel that propels us past momentary setbacks and keeps us moving in the direction of our potential.

When Britain's legendary leader Winston Churchill was asked what his country's greatest weapon had been against Hitler's Nazi regime during World War II, he didn't hesitate for a moment. He promptly replied, "It was what England's greatest weapon has always been—hope."

Hope took England through many dark times during World War II. It can do the same for us today.

Remember some time in your life when somebody or something gave you hope. How did it feel? Did it energize you? Did it revitalize you? Did it provide you with just the burst of belief in better endings you needed to keep trying when quitting seemed the only logical choice? I know hope has done so for me.

During one particular challenging season in my life, when everything I cherished seemed so very close to slipping away, I momentarily lost hope. At a time when I needed to tap a reservoir of deeper inner strength, focus and faith to get me moving in a better direction, I found myself being overwhelmed with fear and frustration. Unsure where to go in an attempt to turn things around, hope seemed lost. Then, just like that, when things seemed at their darkest, one person came into my life who helped me find my way.

Her name was Carol and she helped me rediscover the power of hope.

Carol's encouragement, enthusiasm and belief in me provided the glimmer of possibility I needed to see through the chaos and uncertainty of my momentary situation. Her optimism infused me with the courage and confidence to lean into my circumstances instead of shrinking back from them. And my life has never been the same since.

There is no reason why each of us can't be like Carol and be a messenger of hope to others. Every day we encounter dozens of opportunities to lend a caring and compassionate ear to hear someone else's struggles, or provide a kind word of encouragement or a brief but sincere compliment to someone in our sphere of influence.

It doesn't matter what role you are playing—co-worker, parent, friend, teacher, supervisor, team member, son, daughter, brother, sister, or neighbor—each of us can choose to oxygenate our surroundings with hope.

One more thing about Carol, my personal purveyor of hope in life's toughest season. At the time she reached out to help, she was facing serious struggles of her own. In fact, despite having a young baby, an adoring family and a flourishing faith, she was dying from cancer. At a time when it would be understandable for her to spend her last precious days being fearful or frustrated about her future, she radiated peace, joy and, above all, hope. With the final hours of her life slipping away, she choose to demonstrate by her attitudes and actions her unwavering belief that:

Hope can sustain you;

Hope can refresh you; and,

Hope can propel you.

Don't wait for a crisis in your own life to learn the invaluable life lesson Carol taught me; namely, hope is to your soul what oxygen is to your body. Hope provides us the strength to stand tall after we've taken a fall, it enables us to trust when we are told waiting is a must, and it allows us to endure when circumstances around us seem so very unsure.

Resolve to start a one-person hope epidemic right where you are.

You never know whose life you might just change.

25

Don't Become Worn Out by Weariness

"The greatest weariness comes from work not done."
Eric Hoffer

You are tired.

You are frustrated.

You are weary.

Weary of feeling as though your dreams are impossible to reach.

Weary of being told you don't fit in, won't make the cut or don't have what it takes to play on the team.

Weary of feeling as though no one appreciates the unique gifts, talents and skills you so desperately want to share with the world around you.

Any of this sound familiar?

These are the types of thoughts that mark seasons of weariness in our lives. Weariness is the state of physical, emotional, and spiritual depletion that has been around as long as work and frustration. It's a devastating form of fatigue that threatens to undermine our dreams, kill our creativity, and diminish our impact—a destructive lethargy that insidiously worms its way into every facet of our lives.

If we are completely honest with ourselves, it's likely each of us can think of times when the burden of weariness tugs at us. I'm speaking of those moments in which we find ourselves operating in the present without joy, facing an uncertain future with little courage or are seemingly pursuing a path with no discernable purpose.

Often, we label such seasons of life as storms, trials, challenges, or low points. These are the moments which test us; which stretch us; which threaten to break us; but also which build us. For some of us, we successfully manage to push back on the specter of weariness and, as a result, these difficult experiences are now seen as some of our most formative experiences. That is, hindsight has provided us new eyes to see how the pain of a difficult situation transformed us in some beneficial way.

On the other hand, there are likely remnants of difficult and daunting seasons that continue to weigh on us. Instead of these memories revealing how a particular experience helped set us on a journey of discovery which has enabled us to grow closer to becoming the best possible version of ourselves, we find ourselves still harboring unresolved pain; lamenting over unproductive thoughts, and fretting over unprocessed guilt. Rather than coming to understand how life's darkest storms are often well-disguised opportunities to grow into the fullness of our potential, we have succumbed to lamenting our circumstances instead of appreciating what they can teach us.

Opening the door for weariness to creep into our lives.

The danger of all this is that, instead of recognizing how experimenting, failing, falling, and starting again (only smarter), is what encourages us to become better tomorrow than we may have been today, weariness convinces us to resist change. It compels us to believe it is better (and certainly safer) to keep doing what we have always done rather than risk taking new ground. The consequence of our being lured into such a disempowering cycle, however, is that it causes us to stagnate. And the more we stagnate, the greater the opportunity for the energy stealing, resentment building effects of weariness to set in and undermine the important contribution we have to make to the world.

Let me leave you with a short, true story before I close.

A writer in his fifties had written a manuscript for a book and sent it to several publishers without success. He grew so discouraged by their repeated rejections that, in a moment of weariness, he threw the manuscript into the wastepaper basket. As his wife tried to salvage the manuscript, he told her sternly, "We've wasted enough time on it. I forbid you to remove it from the wastebasket!"

I think you can guess how well that went.

She decided the manuscript should be seen by at least one more publisher. When she arrived at that publisher's office, she pulled out the most unusual looking package that the publisher had ever seen. Underneath a wrapping of brown paper was a wastepaper basket still holding the writer's manuscript. In this way, she reasoned, she was not technically going against her husband's wishes. She did not remove the manuscript. Instead the publisher did it for her when he pulled it from the trashcan.

The publisher read the manuscript and loved it. So he sent an unexpected letter of congratulations to the author of the story, a man named Norman Vincent Peale. The manuscript Peale had tossed in the trash was *The Power of Positive Thinking*. The book has since sold 30 million copies.

Although it is hard to fathom that the very grandfather of the Positive Thinking Movement initially gave up on the book that launched his career, this story should remind us to be wary of falling prey to the devastating form of fatigue that threatens to undermine our dreams, kill our creativity, and diminish our impact. It also should remind us no one is immune to weariness. Everyone at one time or another is tempted to throw in the towel. Don't let that be you. Resolve to move past your momentary weariness. Recognize that harboring old hurts, clinging to past headaches and lamenting over disappointing heartaches will not position you to do your best work.

Commit today to not allow weariness to get the better of you. Convince yourself not to quit when frustration is high and satisfaction is low. You never know; you may be on the verge of producing your greatest work yet.

26

Be Willing to Shake the Tree

"For to be free is not merely to cast off one's chains, but to live in a way that respects and enhances freedom for others."
Nelson Mandela

Not long ago, the world experienced the passing of a leadership icon.

Nelson Mandela was a man who lived his life putting others first—his family, his country, the world. Committed to using every ounce of energy to promote change, his is a timeless example of how a single, persistent person can make a profoundly positive difference, no matter how daunting or discouraging their circumstances.

Of course, no one, including Mandela himself, knew the full impact his actions would one day have on the world. Sentenced to life in prison in the Republic of South Africa on June 12, 1964 for refusing to succumb to the injustice and falsehoods of apartheid, Mandela went into confinement clinging to his belief in the importance of fighting for *truth*. Twenty-six years later, he emerged from prison, set free by none other than what he valued most in his life: *truth*.

Shortly after his release from prison, South African President F. W. de Klerk and Mandela reached an agreement that would help mend the long-standing rift in their country. And on February 2, 1990, the dark veil of apartheid was finally lifted from South Africa, forever.

Despite much rejoicing, many questions lingered. Most related to how the deep wounds of so many years of oppression and hatred could be healed; people questioned how justice could be restored and how a resolution could be achieved.

To some, only one answer seemed logical. Harkening back to an earlier time in world history where atrocities and heartache met the tribunals of justice in the halls of Nuremberg, Germany following World War II, the courtroom seemed the most appropriate place to settle the score. But Nelson Mandela, joined by his friend Desmond Tutu, knew they needed to lead their country on a different path. And why not? After all, his entire life was marked by fighting for truth, sacrificing for truth, and ultimately Mandela was liberated by truth. In his heart, he knew revenge was not only hollow, it would do nothing to kick-start the process of positive change for the nation and its people.

So, instead of fixating on retaliation, he sought reconciliation. Where retribution would only further divide and move people further apart, he believed restoration would unite and bring people closer together. So, in an incredible act of unwavering commitment to leading the change he wanted to see in his surroundings, both Mandela and Tutu chose to deviate from expectations and create the Truth and Reconciliation Commission. All those who would come forward and confess the truth about their apartheid crimes would be set free. They would be granted instant pardon; amnesty was their gift for the taking.

In the history of modern times, perhaps no act of moral courage stands out so clearly or as profoundly as in this one moment. But it was only made possible because of the conviction of a man whose willingness to take a stand for his deeply held ideals and values ensured truth had her most powerful hour.

*   *   *

Today, Mandela's legacy looms large over a world with too few positive role models. His legacy lives in the lessons about leadership he left for all of us. Lessons on the power of collaboration, striving to unite people rather than further divide them, and the importance of not settling for how things are when you know they could be so much more. All this said, perhaps it should be no surprise that Nelson Mandela's African name—Rolihlahla—means *the one who shakes the tree*, the one who unsettles the status quo. It was as if he was born to teach our world the timeless lessons of humility, humor, grace, and above all, standing and fighting for your personal sense of truth—even if it means standing alone.

Instead of mourning Mandela's passing, I believe we would all be wise to consider how we can mirror his positive example on our own surroundings. Imagine how different the world would be if each of us emulated his stated belief that "There is no passion to be found playing small—in settling for a life that is less than the one you are capable of living."

Sadly, I'm convinced that one of the biggest impediments to our actively mirroring Mandela is that our culture routinely reminds us to cast struggle in a negative light—to see hardship as something to be avoided and failure as a sign of weakness. The truth of the matter is, and as the example of Mandela's life bears out, if we opt to view struggle and hardship as something to be shunned, we will relegate ourselves to leading much less rewarding lives than we are capable of experiencing. It will cause us to think in deficit terms, more concerned with what we may lose rather than that which we may gain by marshaling the strength of character needed to endure a transitory season of hardship or pain.

Mandela innately understood many of life's greatest lessons are learned when we lose something we value—our relationships, our careers, our freedoms. In the same way, others-centered leaders know that losing is what makes winning possible. Life is all about learning from the losses, making the right mistakes, fighting the right battles. In fact, the one thing necessary for mirroring a leader like Mandela is to understand it is not that one wins, but that one is willing to risk losing something significant that helps us become the best possible version of ourselves. True leaders understand this. And Mandela was a true leader.

For those of us serious about mirroring Mandela in our own spheres of influence, I offer one final piece of advice: Guard yourself from developing a deficit mindset or the flawed belief that you can only win if others lose. Choose instead to adopt a growth mindset—the belief your abilities are not fixed and innate, but rather acquired over time, honed equally in good times and in tough times.

Individuals who choose a growth mindset choose to look beyond present circumstances and see their challenges not as a measure of who they are today, but instead, consider them an opportunity to become what the world needs them to be tomorrow. Adopting such a view provides new eyes to see as the great Nelson Mandela saw. It allows us to focus on reconciliation where others only see retaliation. It equips us to see restoration when others fixate on retribution. It emboldens us to stand and fight for truth when it is more convenient or comfortable to settle for a life that is less than the one we are capable of living.

In the end, Nelson Mandela showed us how love rather than hate is a more powerful force to promote positive change. He reminded us how great leaders approach life as a school. They are always learning, unafraid to see themselves as a work in progress—allowing the seasons of life to progressively mold them closer to their ideal form.

Commit today not to allow the painful memories of your past to hold you back from the pursuing the possibilities that exists around you. Become a person worth following by fighting for truth, taking on great challenges, risking failure and striving for positive progress. Don't shy away from making mistakes. Choose to mirror Mandela and unsettle the status quo.

Be willing to shake the tree.

EMPOWER

Others-Centered leaders recognize the best use of power is not to have to use it at all. They understand people follow exceptional leaders because they respect them, not because they possess power over them.

27

Have the Courage to Stand Out

"Anyone can achieve their full potential ... but the
path we follow is always of our own choosing."
Martin Heidegger

One of my favorite stories as a child was that of David and Goliath. It is still one of my favorites.

Several thousand years ago, the Israelites and Philistines faced off in battle. David's older brothers were members of the vast army of Israel, while David (the youngest brother) was trusted to stay behind the advancing army and tend the sheep.

One day David's father, Jesse, sent David forward to the war zone to deliver some food to his brothers and to gather some news about how things were progressing. David quickly arranged for others to take care of the sheep while he took off on his mission.

On arriving at the battlefield, David was dismayed to find his brothers and the rest of the Israeli army cowering in fear from the taunts of Goliath of Gath. Goliath was the champion of the Philistine army. He was also a giant of a man, registering about nine feet tall. Hurling scores of disparaging remarks and insults at the Israeli army arrayed around him, he hoped someone would take him up on his offer to engage in battle. But the Israeli army sat paralyzed in fear. No one stepped up to accept Goliath's challenge.

David, watching this disempowering state of affairs continue for several days, became filled with righteous indignation. He decided to do what no one else would; he volunteered to fight the giant. No doubt the king and his advisers must have thought David had lost his mind, or at least harbored a serious death wish. Nonetheless, despite a number of people trying to dissuade him, David refused to back down. He was committed to standing his ground.

Since no one else stepped up to answer the giant's challenge, King Saul offered David his royal armor to wear into battle. David graciously refused the offer, largely because the armor was about two sizes too big, and he knew it would do little more than slow him down in the already very mismatched fight.

From a personal standpoint, I can only imagine the stunned silence on the Israeli side and overt laughter on the Philistine side as the teenage David set out to fight the supersize Goliath on the open field. On his way to the battlefield, David paused to gather five smooth stones from the river and pocketed four of them. The fifth went into the sling prepared for its intended target, Goliath.

As they approached each other, Goliath mocked David, saying he certainly was not afraid of a little boy. David rebutted, boldly declaring that by the end of the day, the birds would be picking the flesh off the giants body. Needless to say, Goliath's inflated ego and swollen confidence told him this young man would be one of his easiest casualties to date.

He was very, very wrong.

History records that as David and Goliath approached each other, David deftly let fly the single stone in his sling. The stone hit the giant between the eyes and sunk into his forehead. Goliath, momentarily incapacitated, fell forward while both armies intently watched the spectacle unfolding before them. David then pulled the giant's own sword (the ultimate "in your face" move if you ask me) and proceeded to chop off the head of the former Philistine champion.

The Philistine army sat there in stunned silence and then tried to make a hasty exit. The Israeli soldiers, energized by the unlikely victory they had just witnessed, used their newfound courage to rout the Philistines before they could escape.

In sum, the final score worked out like this: shepherd boy with the courage to stand his ground–1; intimidating, arrogant, and previously undefeated giant–0.

Game over.

*   *   *

I share this well-known story of David and Goliath with you because it teaches us much more than trying extra hard to overcome seemingly insurmountable odds. It's a story designed to remind us, among other things, of the danger of allowing the voices of the crowd to drown out our belief in our own potential.

As I write at length about in my first book, *(No More) Mediocre Me*, none of us were born to simply blend in with the crowd. We were created to stand out. Every one of us has the spirit of David within us in that we are unique and teeming with a specific array of talents, strengths, and passions capable of being used to promote positive change in our surroundings.

Statistics confirm, however, that despite this amazing and intrinsic ability to stand out, most of us choose to "go along to get along." Instead of celebrating our originality, we opt to play it safe and settle for the commonality found in blending in with the crowd. We dress alike. We sound alike. And when people dare to challenge the prevailing or conventional thinking of the day, we are often guilty ourselves of labeling them as outliers or rabble-rousers, rather than valuing their willingness to stand up and fight for their convictions.

So how can we each push back on this tendency to simply blend in with the masses? Try following these suggestions:

> **Celebrate your own identity:** A popular saying goes, "People laugh at me because I am different; I laugh at them because all of them are the same." Being true to who you are is what

makes you stand out from the crowd. Going along to get along does little more than kill innovation, stifle growth, and hinder you from achieving your goals, hopes, and dreams. Choose to illuminate, liberate, and cultivate your unique strength and then get busy helping those around you do the same.

Press for the offensive: Taking new ground means you have to move forward, not stand still. Ask yourself which meaningful goal or objectives you've quit pursuing. Pick one and commit to do something in the next 24 hours to get back on track. Remember, to flourish in life, you must be willing to go all out and fight for what you believe in—even if it means you have to follow in David's footsteps and take on giant-sized challenges along the way.

Stand your ground: All of us in life at one time or another face our own Goliath-sized struggles. We all experience moments others will tell us we are ill-equipped or incapable of conquering the giant-sized obstacles set before us. Don't buy those lies. Keep in mind, the more conscious you are of your particular talents, strengths, and passions, the more confidence and courage you bring to bear on the choices you must make in your sphere of influence. So the next time you are tempted to follow the masses and toe the line, or get in line, because it's what is easy, choose to hold the line instead.

Never forget none of us were born to blend in; we were all born to stand out. Are you consistently following the path of your own choosing?

28

Always Eye the Exit

*"In any moment of decision, the best thing you can
do is the right thing, the next best thing is the wrong
thing, and the worst thing you can do is nothing."*
Theodore Roosevelt

Have you noticed how the most effective leaders exhibit a sense not of
glamour but of responsibility? They are much less concerned with the
opinions of others than they are with staying true to their personal
sense of truth, inspiring others by their examples, and empowering
others to join them in working toward a worthy common goal.

Such bold, selfless, others-centered leadership implies a willingness
to accept responsibility as much for failure as for success. It reflects an
openness to taking risks and pushing forward into uncharted territory.
And perhaps most importantly, it reveals to us what it looks like to
refrain from allowing ambition to outpace virtue, arrogance to cloud
judgment, or convenience to override character.

Does this description seem too good to be true? After all, I certainly
understand it's much easier to highlight a list of admirable qualities and
desirable traits than it is to actually consistently emulate them. And
I'll be the first to admit identifying a leader with the moral courage to
routinely act with such unshakeable conviction and respectful candor

is rare. But I also know it's possible. Take my personal leadership role model, Theodore Roosevelt, for example.

By any measure, Roosevelt was an incredible man. By his fiftieth birthday, he had completed two terms as president of the United States. He also served in a host of significant capacities, including vice president under William McKinley, New York state legislator, undersecretary of the navy, police commissioner for New York City, and governor of the state of New York. He also achieved the rank of colonel in the US Army.

As president, he was the visionary behind building the Panama Canal, the impetus for placing 230 million acres of land into federal protection as national parks, and the architect of America's world-class naval fleet. President Roosevelt was also the energy behind several pieces of legislation that protected the rights of American workers across a broad range of industries.

If that was not enough, he also ran a cattle ranch in the Dakota territories; served as a reporter and editor for a host of newspapers, journals, and periodicals; and wrote nearly fifty books on a wide array of subjects. He read no fewer than five books a week every week of his life. Theodore Roosevelt is the only president to be awarded both the Nobel Peace Prize and the Medal of Honor, our military's highest decoration for heroism and valor. However, to his dying day, he cited his greatest accomplishments as raising six children and a lifelong romance with his wife.

During his storied career, Roosevelt was hailed by supporters and rivals alike as the greatest man of the age—perhaps one of the greatest of all ages. Even his lifelong political opponent, William Jennings Bryan, conceded Roosevelt was a leader like no other. "Search the annals of history if you will," he said. "Never will you find a man more remarkable in every way."

Despite his widely recognized talent, however, perhaps Roosevelt's most noteworthy trait was his willingness to march to the beat of a different drum—to work and live differently from the many professional politicians of his era, or any era for that matter. Seemingly intent to live his life by the now-famous Nike slogan, "Do Hard Things," he was a leader unafraid to think differently, act boldly, and do something every day to add value to his surroundings.

Admittedly, Roosevelt's style was viewed by many as unconventional. This was largely because many people of his time felt he didn't neatly fit their belief of how he should act—especially as the President of the United States.

And what I find most appealing about this seemingly inconvenient truth is that he liked it that way.

Why, you ask? I don't believe it was because he necessarily wanted to be difficult or particularly disruptive. Rather, I think he innately understood what every successful leader in history has figured out; namely, that it is impossible to truly serve the legitimate needs of others if your unchecked personal ambition causes you to do what is safe rather than what is right.

Roosevelt understood that when leaders get caught up calculating every move they make based on how their actions will impact the next election, influence their popularity or risk tarnishing their reputation, they often avoid challenging the status quo, even when doing so is exactly what is required to improve conditions around them.

Think about it. Where would our nation be today if Roosevelt had not bucked the system and pushed to build the Panama Canal, establish the host of conservation programs we enjoy today (including designation of the Grand Canyon as a national park), invest in building a powerful Navy, and the scores of other significant accomplishments on his watch? Though no one can say for certain, I think it's fair to say we are an immensely better country today as a result of Roosevelt's keen sense of imagination and clear vision of the future.

All this said, I think Roosevelt's true leadership success stemmed from following two basic principles—both of which empowered him to lead boldly and brilliantly and which can help each of us do the same.

The first principle is that he chose to *keep his eye on the exit*, meaning, he intentionally approached each leadership position as though it would be his last. Unlike many politicians past and present who view their current role as a platform to propel them to even greater heights, Roosevelt viewed his present vocation as the most important position he ever held. It was a perspective grounded in his understanding of his own fallibility—an understanding which liberated him to leverage his unique genius while not falling victim to unchecked ambition, runaway pride or self-centered promotion.

The second principle stemmed from his understanding that a system's natural inclination is to encourage leaders to *manage to the middle*. That is, to use power, position and authority to maximize predictability and reduce deviance. The problem with this approach, however, is the middle of the deviance curve is the realm of mediocrity. It's the safe zone that begets a way of leading that prefers to guard the comfortable and the convenient rather than risk doing something different.

The questions I have for you then are, do you treat your current leadership role, be it as a spouse, parent, teacher, platoon leader, or floor manager as the most important position you will ever hold? Are you acting with the courage and conviction that comes from knowing you are willing to do hard things, even when it may be uncomfortable or unpopular? Are you keeping an eye on the exit or are you managing to the middle?

Regardless of how you answer these questions, please remember this: The leaders who succeed in moving things forward in their surroundings always *keep an eye on the exit* and *refuse to manage to the middle*. They abhor mediocrity, avoid hubris and embrace excellence by remaining as indifferent to praise as they are to criticism. They choose to measure their effectiveness by their willingness to accept responsibility for finding creative solutions to persistent problems, even when they have every excuse to find none. And, perhaps most importantly, they recognize that, in any moment of decision, the best thing to do is the right thing, the next best thing is the wrong thing, and the worst thing to do is nothing.

Are you unafraid to think differently, act boldly, and do something every day to add value to your surroundings? Are you up to doing hard things in order to create conditions for others to flourish and thrive?

29

Learn to Fail Forward

"When achievers fail, they see it as a
momentary event, not a lifelong epidemic."
John Maxwell

The world is tough on people who fail. After all, we are taught early on it is best to be a winner. The trophies are shinier; the medals brighter; and the applause louder. Making a name for ourselves and working our way to the top is what it's all about. Right?

Not so fast.

In my almost three decades of leadership experience, I've come to realize progress and success comes in many shapes and takes many forms. In fact, I've come to the conclusion that one of the most valuable but underestimated leadership lessons we must learn if we are to make the most of our influence is to "fail forward".

I first came across the concept of failing forward in a book by leadership expert John Maxwell. He describes the ability to fail forward as being willing to get back up after you've been knocked down, learn from your mistake, and move forward in a better direction. In other words, to fail forward is to learn to see failure as a friend, not a foe. Take the experience of some of history's most successful people as proof.

Vincent Van Gogh failed as an art dealer, flunked his entrance exam to theology school, and was fired by the church after an ill-fated attempt at missionary work. In fact, during his life, he seldom experienced anything other than failure as an artist. Although a single painting by Van Gogh would fetch in excess of $100 million today, in his lifetime, Van Gogh sold only one painting, four months prior to his death. And it sold for less than many of us spend at Starbucks in a week.

Of course, Van Gogh isn't the only famous person who has failed. Before developing his theory of relativity, Albert Einstein struggled academically. In fact, one headmaster expelled Einstein from school and another teacher predicted that he would never amount to anything. Einstein even managed to fail his entrance exam into college.

Prior to dazzling the world with his sensational athletic skill, Michael Jordan was cut from his sophomore basketball team. Despite earning six championships and accumulating a litany of Most Valuable Player and other honors during his professional career, Jordan still missed over 12,000 shots, lost nearly 400 games, and failed to make more than 25 would-be game-winning baskets.

Failure didn't stop Vincent Van Gogh from painting, Albert Einstein from theorizing, or Michael Jordan from playing basketball, but it has paralyzed countless leaders and prevented them from reaching their potential. And failure shouldn't stop you if you are intent in becoming the others-centered leader you are capable of becoming.

So how can you learn to fail forward? I would start by guarding yourself from believing the following mistruths:

Don't Believe Failure is Avoidable. It's Not. You have likely heard the saying, "To err is human, to forgive divine." That was written by Alexander Pope more than 250 years ago, and his words are a reminder that people are prone to making mistakes. Refuse to buy into the notion that mistakes and missteps can be avoided. They can't. Accept that failing is a natural part of pushing your potential and pursuing your dreams.

Don't Believe Failure is The Enemy. It's Not. Most people are so afraid of failure, they try to avoid it like the plague. But in doing so, they fail to recognize it takes adversity to create success. It takes hardship to build endurance. It takes crisis to build character. Musicologist, Eloise Ristad, emphasizes that, "When we give ourselves permission to fail, we at the same time give ourselves permission to excel." She's right. Begin to view failure as a natural byproduct of growing into your full, positive potential.

Don't Believe Failure is Irreversible. It's Not. There's an old saying in Texas that goes, "It doesn't matter how much milk you spill as long as you don't lose your cow." In other words, mistakes are not irreversible. The problems come when you see only the "spilled milk" and not the bigger picture. NBA coach Rick Pitino likes to remind his players, "Failure is good. It's fertilizer. Everything I've learned about coaching I've learned from making mistakes." Failing is simply a natural and necessary part of growing into the best possible version of ourselves.

Don't Believe Failure is Optional. It's Not. According to business professor, Lisa Amos of Tulane University, entrepreneurs fail an average of four times before they finally succeed. They recognize that three steps forward and two steps back still equals one step forward. Don't fall into the trap of thinking failure is optional — it's not. Learn to see your mistakes as stepping stones to success.

At some point, all successful leaders are tempted to believe they are failures. But in spite of that, they persevere. In the face of adversity, shortcomings, and rejection, they hold onto the belief that their dream is still worth pursuing. So much so, that they refuse to see failure as fatal, choosing instead to transform setbacks into comebacks, missteps into next steps, and mistakes into opportunities to start again, only better equipped for the journey ahead.

As John Maxwell reminds us, "the difference between average people and achieving people is their perception of and response to failure." People who allow failure to define them are prone to make the same mistake over and over. Accept you will make mistakes, but don't conclude that you're a failure until you breathe your last breath. Until then, recognize you're still in the process of developing, and there is still time to turn things around for the better.

So take my advice and fail early, fail often, and fail forward. You'll be a better leader and the world will be a better place for it.

30

Embrace the Power of Positivity

"It is our attitude at the beginning of a
difficult undertaking which, more than
anything else, determines its outcome."
William James

On October 16, 2005, an incredible feat was achieved 16 miles west
of Denver, Colorado. What was once considered one of the most
contaminated and environmentally dangerous locations on earth was
reopened to the public as a pristine wildlife refuge in one-sixth the
time and for less than one-sixth the cost of original cleanup estimates.
In tangible terms, a project initially forecast to span 70 years and
cost taxpayers $36 billion was completed 60 years ahead of schedule
and $29 billion under budget, a feat the government's own General
Accounting Office declared unlikely, if not impossible.

In their book, *Making the Impossible Possible: Leading Extraordinary*
Performance: The Rocky Flats Story, Kim Cameron and Michael Lavine
chronicle how in 1989, following years of complaints from workers,
unions, and environmental regulators, the FBI raided the Rocky Flats
nuclear facility and shut it down. Three years later, the facility was
permanently closed by order of President George H.W. Bush.

Shortly thereafter, the Department of Energy conducted a careful
study of the site's residual pollution and concluded that the cleanup

132

and closure of the facility would require a comprehensive effort on a scale that had never been attempted in United States history. Yet less than ten years after beginning the massive cleanup effort, every building at Rocky Flats had been demolished, all radioactive waste had been removed, and all soil and water had been remediated to a level that exceeded federal cleanliness standards by a factor of 13.

In the end, the transformation of Rocky Flats wasn't merely a matter of going from good to great. It was nothing short of altering awful to astonishing. And the best part is it offers all of us a series of compelling leadership lessons on how each of us can promote positive change in our surroundings, one willful choice at a time.

*   *   *

It would have been understandable if everyone charged with sanitizing Rocky Flats had focused on all the challenges that were to be overcome. With scores of contaminated buildings, 5,000 disenfranchised employees, and enormous quantities of weapons-grade nuclear waste, there was no shortage of problems to be tackled. Yet history confirms those charged to lead this change effort chose to spend far less time fixating on all that was wrong and instead opted to channel their energy into creating ways to make things right.

Over the course of the last decade, I have been privileged to lead three massive, multibillion-dollar change efforts myself. In the process, I too have learned that in every organization, something works and change can be proactively and positively managed. Yet as simple as this idea may sound, it's important to understand that this is not our natural approach.

The traditional approach to leading change is to identify a problem, do a diagnosis, and seek a solution. In other words, the primary focus is on what is wrong or broken. This makes sense when we consider most of us have years of practice in the art of problem solving, so we shouldn't be surprised to discover we frequently find exactly what we are looking for: that which isn't working.

Conversely, some of us learn along life's journey the same lesson the leaders of Rocky Flats understood: there is actually greater power, energy, and opportunity in allowing our successes to crowd out the unsuccessful. As psychologist and psychotherapist Carl Jung highlighted, a challenging problem is rarely solved. Instead, it is outgrown, as a newer, stronger interest compels us to direct our attitudes and actions in a more compelling direction. Much like a plant naturally grows toward the light, the fact of the matter is we each yearn to be exposed to positive forms of leadership.

Now, I know the definitions and variations of leadership abound. Yet after a quarter century of studying and, more importantly, applying leadership to a whole host of challenges and opportunities, I've found leading effectively is less about your ability to plan, organize, set a direction, establish a strategy, or execute meticulously. Yes, these things are important and necessary, but they are insufficient in themselves. You see, relying on these more traditional forms of leadership leaves out the most powerful act of leadership there is: equipping, encouraging, empowering, and, ideally, inspiring those around you to use their personal influence to leave the world around them better than they first found it.

The keyword in this personal definition of leadership is positive *influence*, specifically, resolving to do what you can, when you can, and where you can to add tangible value to your surroundings. Those leaders who guided the improbable (and now historical) transformation at Rocky Flats did not succeed because they opted to do more of the same. Rather, they chose to envision a future that was a collage of bests. They effectively instilled in every member of the team that they were each doing something purposeful, meaningful, and important, igniting a cycle of positive change that propelled the organization to heights no one had once thought possible. So how can you use your personal influence to become a more effective, positive leader? I recommend beginning here:

Embody optimism. Positive leaders allow their example to speak for itself. They choose to believe that they will find a way to be successful, even in the face of what seems to be insurmountable obstacles. Hannibal, the great Carthaginian military commander, once said, "We will find a way or make one." Allow your enthusiasm and optimism to compel others to be and do their best.

Elevate morale: Orienting toward the positive goes beyond just a few people doing the right things for the right reasons; it involves everyone within an organization collectively performing in a manner that has an impact on both people and results. Make the most of opportunities in your sphere of influence to communicate and demonstrate compassionate support for those around you. Take time to honor people for their contributions and acknowledge their individual talent. Resolve to do your part to create conditions for every member of your team to flourish, thrive, and come fully alive.

Enhance inquiry: Author and innovation expert Warren Berger reminds us in his wonderful book, *A More Beautiful Question*, that one of the most powerful forces for igniting positive change in business and in our daily lives is the simple, underappreciated tool called inquiry—smart, frequent question asking. Leaders who make it a priority to question deeply, imaginatively, and frequently are more likely to identify and solve problems, come up with game-changing ideas, and view as opportunity what others largely see as obstacles. The leaders of the remarkable Rocky Flats transformation succeeded because they appreciated the value of raising questions no one else was previously asking and discovering powerful answers in the process. Take a page from their playbook and opt to be a leader who assumes less and questions more. Make inquiry your priority.

Value people above things always: Positive leaders are not confused about life's most precious and valuable commodity—healthy, effective, mutually beneficial relationships. Although we certainly need systems, processes, technology, and a host of other tools and platforms to accomplish our goals and objectives, none of these are a suitable substitute for the power of empowered people working toward a common, compelling cause. Never lose sight that as a leader, what stands the test of time isn't the projects you completed, the awards you amassed, or the rank you achieved. What matters more than anything are the lives you touch—for good—along the way. Never, never forget that people are always more important than things.

All of these characteristics have one thing in common: they are contagious. As a leader, you have the opportunity every day to inject energy and passion into your team or organization. You can choose to use your positive influence to do everything in your power to leave the world better than you first found it.

Radioactive waste not required.

31

LEARN to be that Somebody

*"To fear love is to fear life, and those who
fear life are already three parts dead."*
Bertrand Russell

In the year 1540, ten men with no capital and no business plan, but with relentless commitment, built what is today considered the most influential business of its kind. The founders (and those who would follow them) were so successful at everything they did they quickly became confidants and advisors to kings and emperors around the world.

Deeply devoted to the value of lifelong learning, the organization these leaders built has become the largest higher-education network on the planet. With a passion for serving others but no plan on how to run a school, they nevertheless established thirty colleges in less than a decade. Two hundred years later, this number has swelled to seven hundred secondary schools and colleges spread across five of the seven continents.

All of which, mind you, continue to thrive today.

At the same time they were building schools, they were also having a huge influence on the arts and sciences as mathematicians, astronomers, physicians, and mapmakers. In fact, they were the first to successfully cross the Himalayas, to paddle the Blue Nile, and to chart the uppermost parts of the Mississippi River. If that is not impressive enough, they also created the first comprehensive atlas of China and eagerly shared the findings of their global travels with all who were interested.

Today, almost 500 hundred years later, this innovative, others-centered organization, known as the Jesuits, is flourishing. With over twenty-one thousand professionals running two-thousand institutions in more than a hundred different countries, they continue to seek new ways to motivate others to take action and remain as committed as ever to leveraging their love of learning to make good things happen.

*   *   *

Some reading this may be familiar with the Jesuit order; many may not be. Admittedly, I wasn't for a very long time. What I found in studying this fascinating five century old 'corporation' was an inspiring example of a group of people who have committed their lives to becoming the best human beings they can possibly be. Not for selfish gain, mind you, but because they understand a life well lived is a life dedicated to serving humanity—one opportunity to add value to your surroundings at a time.

Admittedly, some of you reading this may wonder what *you* can learn from these unlikely world changers and universe benders. After all, they are members of a religious order that is likely different from your own organization. However, like the Jesuits, I am convinced each of us wants to use our time, talent and energy to help make the world better than we first found it. We, too, want to lead a lifestyle that equips, mentors, trains, and coaches others to become the best possible version of themselves.

I suggest, the same secrets to success the Jesuits employed for the past five centuries to challenge old assumptions and unlock new horizons can also elevate our performance, enhance our effectiveness, and empower us to spend more time looking outside ourselves so we can become more effective at serving those around us. Here are five lessons we can all **L.E.A.R.N.** from these impressive others-centered change agents—lessons that will not only make us more effective leaders, but happier, healthier and more satisfied individuals.

Lead with Your Talents: The Jesuits are driven by an intense desire to add tangible value to their surroundings. They are passionate about their cause and relentless in their drive, but they understand possessing passion without talent is like driving a car without a full tank of gas—it won't get you as far as you want to go. To be truly effective, you must understand your own talents and make it a priority to learn the talents of those around you. The greater your ability to illuminate, activate and celebrate the capabilities of your team, the greater the likelihood you'll enhance everyone's potential for success.

Embrace Excellence: The Jesuits' many amazing accomplishments are not the result of good fortune, chance or luck. Their success is a byproduct of bold goals meticulously planned and deliberately executed. Their impressive results reflect what can be accomplished when people transform their desire to pursue excellence into a way of thinking and being that makes the most of opportunities to promote positive change—a reminder that one of the greatest compliments we can pay someone is to empower them to grow up and into their full potential.

Act with Intentionality: The Jesuits learned long ago the value of intentionally acquiring mastery in their respective area of expertise, anticipating emerging patterns in their surroundings, and finding opportunities to promote progress in pressure situations. They also understand that the most successful leaders challenge the members of their team to think deeply while trusting them enough to make choices that will stretch them in new, and at times, uncomfortable ways. Remind those around you that leadership is largely a learned behavior that becomes unconscious and automatic over time. Challenge them to question whether they like the leader they are becoming.

Refuse to Settle for Good Enough: If one thing rings out loud and clear about the Jesuits' unparalleled success it's that they never stop believing that opportunities exist all around them to elevate the bar on their performance. Throughout my own career, I have made it a priority to seek out bosses, coworkers, mentors and assignments that would help me grow. I've done so even if it meant leaving people scratching their head wondering why I didn't take the 'safe bet' or press forward with the 'sure thing'. Here's why I have continuously pursued the path of less traveled. I know I will never become the leader I want to be, and others deserve to see if I allow myself to settle for good enough when I'm capable of so much more. You won't either. Don't settle. Push past your comfort zone and challenge yourself to be your best you.

Never Let Fear be Your Driving Force: Another reason for the Jesuits' incredible success over the past five centuries stems from their founder Ignatius Loyola's firm belief that the accepted practices of his time were insufficient to bring about positive, lasting change in the world. Remember, Loyola lived in an era when power was controlled by a handful of institutions and, ultimately, consolidated by those who controlled those institutions. Anyone who deviated would be dealt with swiftly and brutally. As such, the majority of individuals in leadership positions chose to leverage fear as a tool to institute compliance and reinforce conformity. But Loyola and his team understood fear constrains people while love, kindness and compassion liberates them. They recognized that fear paralyzes initiative, stifles creativity, and provides no incentive to stretch and to grow. We must recognize the same. Fear is a force dissipater whereas selflessness is a force multiplier.

When Jorge Mario Bergoglio was selected as the 266th pope of the Catholic Church in early 2013, he immediately showed the world his leadership style would be different than those before him. From declining the papal limo and riding the bus, rejecting the traditional red papal slippers and settling for simple black shoes and refusing the opulent apartment in the Apostolic Palace in favor of living in the Vatican guesthouse, the world's first Jesuit pope is demonstrating daily his commitment to becoming the best human being he can possibly be. Not for selfish gain, mind you, but because he understands a life well lived is a life dedicated to serving humanity—one opportunity to add value to your surroundings at a time.

Keep in mind that you don't have to be a pope or belong to a religious order to set an example worth emulating. You just have to be willing to LEARN the lessons of some of the world's most successful change agents and resolve to be someone who can get over themselves in order to serve a purpose greater than themselves.

Ready to be that somebody?

32

Don't be a Faint-Hearted Leader

*"The greatest test of courage is to bear
defeat without losing heart."*
Robert Green Ingersoll

A tale from the Far East tells of a mouse that was so terrified of cats he would rarely risk stepping out into the world.

One day, a local magician agreed to transform the terrified mouse into a cat. This curtailed his fear and the mouse-turned-cat was happy.

That is, until he met a dog.

Now terrified of dogs, the mouse-turned-cat rarely refused to step out into the world. Yet again, the magician agreed to turn him into what he feared most—a dog.

With his latest fear now gone, the mouse-turned-cat-turned-dog was happy.

That is, until he met a lion.

So, once more, the magician agreed to turn the mouse into what he now feared the most—a lion.

Not a week later, the mouse-turned-cat-turned-dog-turned-lion came complaining to the magician that he had met a hunter and was once again afraid. However, this time the magician refused to help him, saying, "I will make you a mouse once again, for though you have the body of a lion, you still have the heart of a mouse."

Does this tale sound familiar to you? Who might you know who has built a formidable exterior in order to hide a fearful interior? Have you come across any leaders in your career who found it hard not only to *make* tough decisions, but also to step up and *own* those decisions? How many leaders have you known who have the *roar* of a lion in public but the *heart* of a mouse in private?

Sadly, I think all of us have encountered people along the way whose fears and insecurities keep them from being the leaders they are capable of becoming—leaders who lack the courage to match their proverbial 'talk' to the reality of their 'walk'; men and women who, like the mouse in our story, are content with coming up with countless excuses not to act when doing so is unsettling, uncomfortable, or just plain risky.

Generally, when we think of courage, the words *bravery* or *valor* come to mind. This is for good reason, as these words describe the type of courage that's easiest for us to see—frequently portrayed on the nightly news in stories of soldiers selflessly serving their country in harm's way in such places as Afghanistan and Iraq, or of firemen risking their own well-being to save the life of a total stranger, or of a police officer apprehending a dangerous felon who means harm to others.

This type of visible courage then reflects *the willingness to act despite the potentially paralyzing fear of injury or death.* In other words, it provides us with the *physical fortitude* to fight for what's right, no matter the potential cost to self.

But each and every day in our personal and professional lives, we are afforded opportunities to exercise a different form of courage. Philosophers, theologians, and ethicists like to term this the courage of our convictions or, more commonly, *moral courage.*

Moral courage, in the words of Rushworth Kidder and Martha Bracy of the Institute for Global Ethics, is "the quality of mind and spirit that enables someone to face ethical dilemmas and moral wrongdoings firmly and confidently, without flinching or retreating." Unlike physical courage, which can be displayed equally by those who strive to live honorably and those who do not, moral courage is only exemplified by those who possess the *internal strength of character* to do what's right, no matter the potential cost to self.

Of course, understanding what moral courage is and actually positioning ourselves to act courageously when facing uncomfortable, unsettling or just plain undesirable situations are two very different things. This is why, years ago, I developed a simple series of questions I ask myself each time I find myself tempted to have the *roar* of a lion in public but the *heart* of a mouse in private.

What am I Scared of Losing? This may seem a simple question, but we often go through life making choices without fully understanding the real motivation for what we are doing. By getting into the habit of taking a moment to genuinely reflect on what we fear we might lose by deciding to act, we help guard ourselves from making short-sighted choices which may result in our leading lives far smaller and narrower than we are capable of living.

What is postponing action costing me financially, emotionally and physically? Bringing to light what opportunities we will forgo or what it will tangibly cost us to stick with the status quo is proven to be one of the most effective ways to get us to risk moving in a new direction. The simple process of assessing the impact of a missed opportunity challenges us to explore whether our rationale for not acting is primarily the result of trying to rationalize away our fear of change or guard ourselves from stepping out in a direction we will likely one day regret.

So What? I've repeatedly found that the secret to routinely exercising the courage to be honest with myself about what is holding me back from doing what I know in my heart to be right in the moment is the willingness to adopt a broader perspective of the situation. By consistently challenging myself to focus equally on all that could go right instead of just fixating on everything that might go wrong, I find I'm better equipped to accept responsibility for taking the initiative to lead the change I want to see occur around me.

Over 2,500 years ago, Chinese philosopher Mencius said that courage is an ideal that should fuel all people's desire and ability to live a life of purpose and meaning. Plato and Socrates considered courage to be not only one of the four cardinal virtues essential to leading a life of unmatched character, but also the grand virtue that made living an honorable life possible. Now I'm no fancy philosopher, but I certainly consider myself a leader and, as such, am committed to ensuring my proverbial 'talk' matches the reality of my 'walk'.

How about you?

33

Watch Your Words

"No act of kindness, no matter how small, is ever wasted."
Aesop

'Sticks and stones may break my bones but words will never hurt me.' Many of you will remember this popular rhyme from elementary school. In fact, you may have even recited it a number of times as kids as it's a common childhood idiom we use to remind people they cannot hurt us with the bad things they say or write about us. Well, now that we're all a little older (and ideally a little wiser), we know that this isn't quite true.

Words have derailed political campaigns, ruined marriages, started wars, and destroyed businesses. Words are a very powerful tool which can either diminish us or inspire us. So much so, in fact, that cognitive scientists tell us emotionally loaded words quickly attract attention, and bad words (war, hate, crime) attract attention faster than happy words (peace, love, joy). In a paper titled, *Bad is Stronger than Good,* researchers report overwhelming evidence that "bad emotions, bad parents, and bad feedback have more impact than good ones, and bad information is processed more thoroughly than the good." How you communicate, the words that comes out of your mouth as a leader, makes an immense difference – for good, or bad.

Take the story of Gene Mauldin. Mauldin grew up in a home in which he was told he would amount to nothing. He heard it so much that he began believing every word. Only after he was blinded during the Vietnam War did a leader in Gene's sphere of influence effectively communicate that he was loaded with talent. Invigorated with a new found confidence in himself, Mauldin went to college, eventually graduating with honors. He then started a construction company that eventually became one of St. Louis's top homebuilders.

Mauldin never forgot that the springboard to his success was one leader's genuine words of affirmation – words that equipped him to see his potential even after he lost his sight.

*   *   *

You hear it all the time ... people hungry to become better leaders want to know the most effective thing they can do to elevate their performance and enhance their influence. They want to discern the key to business success. Thinking the answer must be something like maximizing technological innovation, savvy marketing, or pursuing far-sighted financial planning – all of which are important – people's jaws drop when I affirm the most important dimension of great leadership is clear and affirming communication.

Think about it. How do the best leaders motivate and inspire their people? Through coherent and compelling communication. How do the best organizations promote discipline, accountability and strategic alignment? With clear communication. And, how do market leaders sell their products and services? With compelling ads and well developed marketing campaigns – in sum, by clear, positive communication. The point itself is crystal clear: In real estate, the old cliché is "location, location, location." In effective leadership, the mantra is "communication, communication, communication."

Of course, not all forms of communication are created equal.

In a fascinating study of 60 top management teams who were engaged in an annual strategic planning, problem solving, and budget setting summit, researchers set out to determine what made some teams perform better than others. Communication experts were then brought in to analyze the team member's interactions.

At end of the evaluation, a single element emerged as the most important factor in predicting the team's performance—positive statements! That's right. Those workgroups that routinely communicated using positive statements, by intentionally expressing appreciation, support, helpfulness, or sharing compliments, significantly out-performed those who used either negative statements (such as expressing dissatisfaction, cynicism or criticism) or sparingly used positive language. In fact, the results of the research revealed that the highest performing teams had a ratio of positive to negative statements of 5.6 to one. That's over five times more positive statements were made to every negative statement.

In contrast, the ordinary teams (read average) had a ratio of 1.85 to one. That's about two positive phrases for every negative phrase used. And here's the eye-opener. In the lowest performing teams, the ratio was a mere .36 to one. In other words, for every one positive statement, three negative statements were made!

Of course, this doesn't mean we should never have negative interactions. In fact, research by Barbara Fredrickson of the University of Michigan shows we can actually overdo positive phrases. When the ratio climbs to 13 to one or greater, we've moved from high performing to high conformity. In these environments, people are not confronting challenging situations, they are avoiding them. And in doing so, allowing mediocrity to own the day.

So please remember this. Our words matter, more than you may have ever thought. So much so, in fact, studies show that leaders who intentionally work to maximize positive communication experience a host of advantages, including increased job satisfaction, greater engagement, and enhanced performance. So the next time you're tempted to believe that 'sticks and stones may break one's bones but words will never hurt them,' think again. Your words, it turns out, possess immense power. They can cut like a sharp knife that wounds and destroys, or serve as a soothing balm that heals and brings life.

The bottom line? Clear, compelling, positive communication is paramount to individual and collective success. Choose your words wisely and watch those around you flourish, thrive and come fully alive. Work at reducing the negativity that escapes from your lips. Let positive communication be your trademark.

34

Cure Your Emotional Poison Oak

"The Past has no power over the present moment."
Eckhart Tolle

Poison oak thrives in the Pacific Northwest. If allowed to grow unchecked, it is capable of taking over acres of fields and forests, rendering the land virtually impossible for people to enjoy. When poison oak is present, even simple excursions such as picnics, hiking, hide-and-seek and a friendly game of family touch football are not worth the risk. If your skin comes into contact with poison oak you'll be miserable for days. And, mowing it down only provides short-term help because, as long as the roots remain, it's guaranteed to return within weeks or months, usually stronger and more widespread than ever.

In many regards, poison oak serves as a great metaphor for those feelings and emotions in life that prevent us from being the best possible version of ourselves. For example, when we've been hurt or wronged in some way, the conditions are ripe for the poison oak of bitterness, frustration, anger and, ultimately, judgment to grow. Left unchecked, these negative thoughts and feelings will begin to spread, first in our own lives and then, quite often, they'll spill over to affect our relationships with others.

Unfortunately, what too few people seem to realize is that, the longer we allow emotional poison oak to take root in our lives, the less effective we become at accomplishing our goals and objectives. After all, life is a team sport, not a solo endeavor. Who wants to be around someone who, like poison oak, makes us feel miserable?

So what's the remedy? We must learn not to harbor ill feelings, develop grudges or internalize our frustrations and disappointments we have with others. After all, human beings are far from perfect. Very few people ever intend to do or say something that is meant to intentionally harm or hurt someone else. Hence, the most effective way to prevent the emotional equivalent of poison oak from spreading in our lives is to always believe the best, seek the best, and give our best. Here are three proven ways to help make this possible:

Take careful notice of your thoughts and emotions: In his book, *The Power of Now*, Eckhart Tolle tells us to be the watcher of our thoughts. What he suggests is that, instead of trying to change our thoughts, we need to pay more attention to our thoughts without getting caught up in them.

We are not the sole creator of our own feelings. When we find ourselves harboring negative feelings or fixating on troubling situations, we can easily lose sight of the fact that what we are facing is but one moment in a very long string of experiences that make up our existence. This is why it is important to develop the habit of periodically pausing and taking notice of what is really going on around us. By taking the time to be a little more aware of our context and our surroundings, we learn to momentarily separate ourselves from our thinking and, over time, our negative feelings and emotions will lessen and greater awareness, grace and acceptance will grow in their place.

Seek to settle scores positively by living and loving well. Allowing the emotional poison oak of resentment to grow unchecked in our lives will almost always lead us to contemplate revenge. But revenge is a one way trip to greater heartache and hurt. Retribution brings zero value into our life. Instead, we should focus on ways to seek to settle scores positively by living and loving others as well as we possibly can.

Now I'll be the first to admit this is not always easy. But if you pause and think about how little good has come from those times you've pursued revenge, I suspect you will find very few (if any) examples of when revenge was a healthy, productive alternative. Remember, devising some strategy to get revenge on someone else will never ease your own inner angst. In fact, it will likely only make things worse.

The way to liberate ourselves from becoming prisoners of the pain of the past is not by pursuing vengeance, mockery, bullying or retaliation, but to do our best to remind ourselves there is always something good we can do. There is always love we can give. We just have to be willing to take the courageous first step forward to do so.

See missteps for what they are ... opportunities for people to stretch and grow. As author Marc Chernoff writes, "Mistakes are the growing pains of wisdom. Most of the time they just need to be accepted, not forgiven."

When we willfully work to see life's turbulent moments as opportunities to find greater inner strength, develop new skills and be more gracious to those around us, there is an obvious shift that occurs in our heart and mind. Instead of believing the worst, we begin to always seek the best ... both in ourselves and in those around us.

Noble Laureate Desmond Tutu tells us in his book, *No Future without Forgiveness*, how in generously forgiving others, we are not asked to forget, nor are we condoning what has been done. Forgiving means "...taking what happened seriously and not minimizing it; drawing out the sting in the memory that threatens to poison our very existence... Forgiving means abandoning your right to pay back the perpetrator in his own coin, but it is a loss that liberates the victim." Without forgiveness, there is no future. Without forgiveness, there is no growth.

Educator, counselor and behaviorist Dr. Bill Gothard, who spends a great deal of time with troubled youth addressing the importance of granting forgiveness, recounts that, in 90% of cases where someone is experiencing psychological, emotional and spiritual travails, bitterness and unresolved hurts is the source of the problem. He adds that the only way to stop this painful, often destructive cycle is to pull out its root—and that can only be done if we choose to generously forgive those who offend or hurt us.

Do you have any emotional poison oak in your life at this moment? If you want relief, perhaps you should try the healing balm of believing the best, seeking the best, and committing to give your best. After all, everyone benefits, especially yourself, for your making such a selfless choice.

35

Remember, You Were
Born to Matter

*"The measure of a life is not what that life accomplishes
but rather the impact that life has on others."*
Jackie Robinson

In September 1944, 9,000 American troops stormed ashore on the tiny island of Peleliu, believing their efforts were critical to our nation's victory in the Pacific.

As it turns out, they weren't.

We now know the assault on this tiny landmass, which was one of the bloodiest battles of World War II with 8,500 Americans being killed or wounded, was simply unnecessary. The selfless contributions of these brave service members were, for all practical purposes, deemed by history *irrelevant*.

But it wasn't supposed to be that way.

Earlier that year, General Douglas MacArthur, the commander of all Allied forces in the Pacific, had designed a strategy to reclaim the Philippines so the United States could use the country as a springboard to invade Japan. This approach entailed conquering a succession of small islands between Hawaii and the Philippines, building runways, and then systematically attacking remaining Japanese strongholds. Peleliu was one of these small islands.

However, while American forces were engaged in ferocious combat with 12,000 well-fortified Japanese soldiers on this tiny volcanic outcropping, the war simply passed them by; scores of other friendly forces were already landing just south of the Philippines with little to no resistance.

In terms of death per square mile, Peleliu was the bloodiest battle of World War II. But, as I mentioned earlier, it was all for nothing. It was the right cause but the wrong fight. These brave soldiers' sacrifice did little to promote the cause of freedom. Their effort, though noble, effectively served no higher purpose. It didn't seem to matter.

*　　*　　*

Each and every one of us wants to know who we are and that what we do has value. We yearn to know that our lives are contributing to something larger than ourselves. In fact, every single person you will ever meet shares this common desire. They want to know they matter.

How can you tell that your life matters and that what you are doing is helping to move things forward in your surroundings? Take this simple yes/no quiz and see for yourself:

- Do you love the work you do and the people you do it with?
- Do you believe that when you leave this world you will have done your part to leave it a better place than you found it?
- Do you routinely raise the bar on what you do and how you do it?
- Do you give, teach and forgive more than you take, tell or rush to judge and demean?
- Does the room brighten when you walk in?
- Are people's lives enriched for having known you?

Did you get more yeses than no's? If so, congratulations. You are living your life with meaning, purpose and passion. If you have more no's, then maybe it's time to rethink what you are doing and why you are doing it.

Napoleon, at the height of his glory and fame, wrote to his brother Joseph, "I am tired of glory at twenty-nine; it has lost its charm; and there is nothing left for me but complete egotism." I believe that, at some point in our journey, most of us will awaken to the reality that living life simply to satisfy our own selfish desires will leave us feeling like Napoleon: empty, frustrated, and deflated—devoid of real meaning.

The brave warriors in World War II who fought so bravely at Peleliu believed their cause mattered and that the blood spilled and effort expended counted for something. Although history now deems their campaign irrelevant, it doesn't diminish the fact that these courageous souls gave everything they had to do what they believed was important. Though it was the wrong fight, it was the right cause.

The priceless cause of securing and defending freedom.

Remember, you were born to matter. Mattering is your birthright, just as mattering is a choice. We can give ourselves that option every day. It doesn't matter how you do it—it only matters that you do it. You can say it, write it, tweet it, or live it. Choose to matter by doing something to make a positive difference in your surroundings. You never know; the ripple effect of your actions could last for generations.

36

Don't Be a Fainting Goat

*"Do what you feel in your heart to be right-
-for you'll be criticized anyway."*
Eleanor Roosevelt

Goats are interesting creatures. But those afflicted with congenital myotonia are especially fascinating.

I suspect you are likely unfamiliar with the medical term, but you may well have seen the videos. The so-called 'fainting goats' are an internet sensation. When frightened or startled, these goats don't run away. They simply seize up and fall over. It's a genetic condition that is generally harmless to goats living in captivity and humorous for their owners. It's conversely a potentially lethal malady for goats living among predators.

Folklore traces the origin of the fainting goat to the 1880s in Marshall County, Tennessee. It's believed that a man by the name of Tinsley came to town bringing along a few 'special' goats and a single 'sacred' cow. As the story goes, he stayed around long enough to marry a local woman and to help a farmer with the harvest. Eventually he sold his goats to a man by the name of R. Goode and then departed the community.

*   *   *

What made these Tinsley goats so 'special' is that they were very effective at protecting livestock. You see, it turns out these particular goats had a habit of literally freezing in place or falling over when a herd of coyotes, wild dogs or other predators threatened the sheep. Conveniently, this allowed the sheep to run away unharmed as the now paralyzed goat provided the predator with an easy meal.

Now you're probably wondering what this funny phenomenon (unless you're the goat, of course) has to do with leadership. So here's my point. I find it serves as a powerful metaphor for one of the biggest personal leadership traps of all; that is, allowing ourselves to become frozen in place by indecision.

Please indulge me for a minute. How often have you experienced a leader who, the minute they face an issue that is challenging, unsettling or just plain uncomfortable, simply locks up? In other words, they faint in the face of hardship, difficulty, or controversy. Instead of accepting responsibility for dealing with the situation at hand head on, they go the way of the fainting goat and freeze. Unsure or unwilling to do anything to get or keep things moving, they opt to do nothing—bringing progress to a literal standstill.

Now ask yourself this question. How many times do you find yourself unwittingly acting like a fainting goat? Are you prone to avoiding making decisions? Are your actions, or lack thereof, keeping you from achieving your goals or accomplishing your objectives? Is fear keeping you from being the leader you want to be and others deserve to see?

If you answered yes to any of these questions, here's some good news. It's not too late to turn things around.

In practical terms, we fall prey to the fainting goat phenomenon for a host of reasons. For instance, we allow ourselves to get overly fixated on a certain worrisome concern and cannot let it go, or we convince ourselves to dwell on risks and imagine the worst, allowing our fear of making a poor choice to convince us not to act at all. Regardless of the reason why we act like a fainting goat, what's important to recognize is that we don't have to stay trapped in this vicious cycle of worry, anxiety and unfounded fear.

So what can we do about it? Try starting here:

Give yourself permission to be less than perfect. Analysis paralysis keeps us playing small. Because it's easy to fall into the trap of wanting everything to be perfect or trying to avoid criticism, it is easy to encode ourselves with all the reasons why we should defer making a decision. Don't do it. Decide today to make informed action your ally and perfection your enemy. And watch your leadership effectiveness increase and your sense of accomplishment soar as a result.

Risk being wrong. Decisiveness means taking the risk that we may be wrong while keeping in mind that perfect clarity is rarely a reality. So recalibrate how you look at risk. Recognize it for what it is: the price of admission for doing your best to move things in a better direction. The next time you find yourself facing a tough decision, gather the facts, seek appropriate advice, and don't be afraid to take the leap.

Know you can't please everyone. This is one of the hardest obstacles to overcome as a leader. After all, it's natural to want to be liked by those around you. The challenge that arises, however, is you can quickly find yourself trapped in a cycle of indecision if you try to please or pacify everyone. That's why the sooner you recognize it's impossible to keep everyone happy, the better. Leading effectively demands you make some unpopular decisions. So stand your ground, remain respectful, but don't abdicate responsibility for acting when it's clearly your place to do so. Others are counting on you to do the right thing.

Reaching your full positive potential as a leader isn't easy. And it's made all the more daunting when you are routinely thrust into positions requiring you to venture outside your comfort zone. Let me be clear. Decisiveness is the key to leadership effectiveness. Achieving results, especially in the face of complexity or uncertainty, comes with the territory. So the next time you find yourself tempted to be frozen in place by indecision, choose instead to weigh the information available and then use your best judgment to choose among the possibilities, recognizing that by your willingness to make a decision you're fulfilling your fundamental responsibilities as a leader.

Show the world you're a leader you can be counted on. Reveal by your attitudes and actions you are someone who can be trusted. Demonstrate by your example that you're certainly no fainting goat.

37

Risk Reaching Out

"Act as if what you do makes a difference. It does."
William James

In the early months of the First World War, millions of servicemen, believing this would be a quick war, rushed from all over the continent to join in the fight. By December of 1914, most realized they had been wrong. This war was far from over. So each side dug miles and miles of trenches across the French countryside, with often only 60 yards separating the combatants. This area between the trenches became known as 'no-man's land'.

As Christmas Day neared, soldiers on both sides began receiving gift boxes containing food and tobacco prepared by their governments. The leaders in Germany sent small Christmas trees and candles to troops at the front. Even Pope Benedict XV intervened, proposing a Christmas cease-fire. Yet his proposal was rejected by both sides as 'impossible'.

Or so everyone thought.

On Christmas Eve, German soldiers unexpectedly set their trees on the trench parapets and lit Christmas candles. They then began singing carols. Though their language was strange, the tune they sang was quite familiar even to their enemies across the dreaded 'no man's land'.

In a matter of minutes, the British decided to join in. Shortly thereafter, soldiers on both sides started raising signboards up and down the trenches with the most oft-repeated German message being: 'YOU NO FIGHT, WE NO FIGHT.' Some British units responded by posting their improvised 'MERRY CHRISTMAS' banners.

As time ticked by, more and more placards popped up. A spontaneous truce resulted. Soldiers from both sides willfully left their trenches, meeting in the middle of 'no-man's land' to shake hands. They even exchanged gifts of chocolate cake, cognac, postcards, newspapers, and tobacco.

By Christmas morning, 'no man's land' had become 'every man's land' as the space between the trenches was filled with fraternizing soldiers, sharing rations and gifts, singing and taking the time to honor their fallen comrades. After some time, a game of soccer was started using improvised balls. It was reported the Germans won with a score of 3-2.

As the day progressed, men continued to exchange gifts and buttons and soldiers who had been barbers in civilian life provided free haircuts. One German, a juggler and a showman, even gave an impromptu performance of his routine in the center of 'no-man's land'. As the sun prepared to set that Christmas Day, commanders on both sides found their troops hesitant to return to their positions and had to order their men to their respective trench under penalty of court martial.

The German and British soldiers reluctantly parted. In the words of Pvt. Percy Jones of the Westminster Brigade, "with much hand-shaking and mutual goodwill," the two sides went their own ways.

After the impromptu cease-fire, German and Allied commanders tried to cover up what had happened. Some generals felt this unauthorized spontaneous truce was treasonous behavior. Even many years after peace interrupted the war, French generals still couldn't fathom why their soldiers deliberately disobeyed orders and joined the German enemy on the silenced battlefields for a forbidden Christmas truce; unable to understand what could move men to climb out of their trenches, put down their weapons and embrace their enemies, if even for a moment.

*   *   *

As the story of the French and German soldiers and their unexpected Christmas truce affirms, when we choose to make the most of our current situation, we gain courage and confidence to stand up for what we believe in. When we pause to do something nice for someone, be it friend or foe, we show we can change the world. Maybe not the whole world, but their world.

So I offer the next time your difficult circumstances try to lull you to take cover in the safety of your own proverbial trench, remember the Battlefield Miracle of 1914. Choose to be a force for good in your surroundings. Risk reaching out in some meaningful way to those around you.

Start small.

Start now.

Here's how:

1. Smile when you make eye contact with someone.
2. Compliment someone's appearance. Flatter them, genuinely.
3. Leave encouraging post-it notes on someone's computer monitor or in random places.
4. Be a connector. Introduce friends or colleagues, on line or in person, to others with shared interests.
5. Commit to living each moment with enthusiasm.
6. Eliminate the words 'hate', 'can't', and 'won't' from your vocabulary.
7. Treat everyone with the same level of respect you'd give to your mother.
8. Ask someone for their opinion or advice.
9. Generously spread praise. Repeat something nice you heard about someone else.
10. Help someone get active. There's a coworker or acquaintance in your life who wants to get healthy, but needs a helping hand. Offer to go to the gym together.

As you will notice, none of these suggestions are complicated; none of them cost money; and none of them matter if you are serving in a war zone or are safely settled at home. They are all small, simple ways to apply the same lesson learned from those courageous soldiers who defied the status quo and facilitated the Battlefield Truce of 1914; namely, never underestimate the power of small acts of kindness and consideration to transform 'no man's land' into 'every man's land'.

Remember, we all have a choice. We can choose to fight or be friendly. We can choose how we respond to others. Even when defending our individual and collective freedoms, we can choose to call a truce during our most daunting circumstances.

Choose to act as if what you do makes a difference. It does.

38

Liberate Your Inner Superhero

"Fate rarely calls upon us at the moment of our choosing."
Optimus Prime

Early in my tenure as Commanding General of NATO Air Training Command—Afghanistan, I had the opportunity to sit down with my aide-de-camp, Sergio Fontanez. Our conversation that day quickly turned from routine matters of scheduling, required phone calls, and the necessary events of the day into a conversation about Serge's fascination with the power of superheroes to teach children valuable life and leadership lessons.

Admittedly, I was a bit skeptical at first. Call it ignorance or lack of imagination, I have to admit I never really gave much thought to what those colorful characters with larger than life capabilities could teach us. Nor had I really considered why superheroes are particularly important to children. So over the next couple hours, Sergio took me to school about the deeper symbolism behind those characters I've known since I was five years old—Batman, Superman, Spider-Man, and a host of others. In the process, he awakened a deeper understanding and appreciation for how the subtle but significant message communicated by these superheroes' examples can liberate each of us, old and young alike, to become the very best version of ourselves possible.

*   *   *

Since their inception in the 1930's, superheroes have always fascinated children. And why not? After all, stories of larger than life heroes saving the day and making our world a little bit safer, better and brighter stirs something in us. Their example *liberates children's imagination* and *inspires them to want to do the right thing*, and to try to leave the world better than they found it.

In many ways, superheroes give children a glimpse of what it looks like to attain their *full potential*. They remind young people how we each possess a special talent or skill that, if we choose, can be selflessly employed in some new or novel way to overcome obstacles, promote progress and remind us we are all powerful in our own right.

Alongside parents and teachers, superheroes also teach children other important life lessons. For example, they show children a way of life that is *morally good*. These heroes do the right thing, not for personal gain but because it is the right thing to do. Spider-Man fights crime not expecting a reward but because criminals need to be stopped; Superman can't be turned from good; Batman refuses to harm innocents even if it means losing the villain.

Of course, superheroes are not without their flaws. As authors Tom Morris and Jeph Loeb remind us, "There can be darkness in a character as well as light, as there is in any human life, but that darkness must ultimately be constrained by the good..." It's important for children to see that superheroes have flaws in order for them to learn how these heroes deal with them. This allows children to understand that nobody is perfect and that everyone has issues that they need to handle in their lives. It enables them to realize it is okay to struggle, to fear and to fall short of their best. It reminds them of the value of not giving up on their beliefs, goals and dreams, regardless whether they fail the first, third or twenty-third time.

Watching superheroes deal with suppressing their inner demons and still commit to fighting for what is right teaches children about self-discipline. It also affirms how power without self-control is dangerous.

This can be seen by taking a look at the antithesis of the superhero, the super villain. These are characters that every superhero fights. Take Superman's nemesis, Lex Luthor, as an example. He uses his superior intellect to create destructive weapons. He also does it strictly for personal gain. These characters are examples of what happens when power goes to your head.

Here is my most important take away from my conversation with Sergio: It's never too late for adults to acquire and emulate our own superhero qualities. I'm now more convinced than ever that we each possess an inner superhero—a person of strength and conviction, of perseverance and commitment, one of character and decency—that the world needs to see. But such power and potential won't always be liberated naturally. It's our job to release the latent talent already there, dormant perhaps, but waiting to be discovered, developed and deployed.

Not sure how to get started? I recommend you begin by reflecting on these four essential characteristics of the typical superhero:

Become Invisible to Fear and Insecurity: We don't need x-ray vision to see through walls of fear and self-doubt. We don't have to possess a cape, wings or special powers to fly above gossip, rumor and innuendo. We can break through the invisible barriers of fear and insecurity by committing to take the high road instead of the easy road. We can choose not to be petty and small and set an example worth emulating. We can opt to shine a bright light into those dark places, and do what's right *even though* we're nervous about taking that step.

Don't be too quick to Judge Yourself or Others: It's tempting to fall into the trap of judging ourselves or others by what we see on the surface, ignoring the potential that shines just below skin-level. Take Batman: who would believe the uber-wealthy, party happy socialite Bruce Wayne is also the selfless and fearless guardian of Gotham City? Who would guess that behind Clark Kent's thick glasses lies a powerful ability to see through walls and across vast distances we cannot fathom? Here's my point. Though we may feel and look ordinary to others, we all have within us some unique, extraordinary gift and skill no other person on Earth possesses. We all have something with one-of-a-kind beauty to share with the world. Some of us just need more time and often, a little help, to discover it.

Take Responsibility for Your Gifts: The only way to make your greatest possible contribution to your surroundings is to accept responsibility for exercising your full talent, gift and skill. Winston Churchill said, "*Responsibility is the price of greatness.*" That means you need to own who you are and what you do. Take every opportunity to put your personal superpowers to the test and watch your confidence climb, your influence soar and the opportunities to add tangible value to the lives of those around you multiply.

Prepare to Meet Some Adversaries: Just as every superhero has a cast of villains to fight, be ready to face resistance in becoming your best you. The good news is you need not fear being chased by laser shooting scoundrels or mutated creatures with extraordinary strength. Your true adversaries will be negative, small minded or jealous people who are intimidated by what you have to offer. Don't allow yourself to be distracted by naysayers or fall prey to the host of excuses for why you shouldn't attempt bold things. Stay focused on your cause and recognize experiencing resistance is a sure sign you are making positive progress.

Just as in comic books, real life can be big, bad and scary. Our challenges can loom large and sometimes seem more daunting than mere mortal flesh and blood can overcome. But don't be fooled. Everything we need to prevail against these fears is already instilled within us. We all possess the power to stand as beacons of hope and healing to the lost, the broken, and the fearful. Just as Clark Kent has a superman inside and Peter Parker is only a web-throw away from Spider-Man, so you and I have amazing powers for good waiting to be tapped.

Cape or costume optional.

39

Leave the World Better
Than You Found It

"Do not wait for leaders; do it alone, person to person."
Mother Teresa

Seven-year-old Lucy Mixson had never seen a homeless person, until she met Charlie.

Charlie was a little rough around the edges. He wore a tattered sweater, stained jeans, and an oversize baseball cap that was tilted slightly to one side. Yet, despite his well-worn external features, Charlie sported a smile that could melt the hardest of hearts. He radiated a joy that seemed displaced given his current predicament.

The chance encounter between Lucy and Charlie one sunny Saturday morning didn't last long. Lucy was running errands with her mom when she pointed to Charlie sitting on a bench and asked, "Mommy, who's that?" Lucy's mom politely looked at Charlie and said, "He is a homeless man."

A puzzled look furrowed Lucy's small face. "What's homeless?"

A little embarrassed, Lucy's mom suddenly realized she had never explained homelessness to her daughter. It wasn't so much a matter of sheltering, as it was simply a subject that had not come up.

Trying to keep her explanation simple, she shared, "There are men, women, and even children who don't have homes, so they do the best they can to find some place to sleep. They sleep with their coats over them and make do with what they have. Some even stay in special shelters called rescue missions."

Lucy reflected on those words for a moment. Then she said, "Can we go by and say hello to the homeless man on the bench?" Though admittedly a bit uncomfortable, her mom agreed but insisted they only stop for a moment.

Walking hand-in-hand, Lucy and Mom strode steadily toward the man with the tattered sweater, stained jeans, and oversize baseball cap tilted slightly to one side. As they arrived within several feet of where he was sitting, young Lucy wasted no time in introducing herself. "Hello, my name is Lucy. My mom says you are homeless. How can I help?"

Lucy's mom was horrified. Charlie, however, was not. Extending his hand and dialing up his smile, he simply replied, "Ms. Lucy, my name is Charlie, and you have already helped. Just you coming by to say hello has brightened my day. You see, not many people take a moment to notice I'm here. Even fewer go out of their way to see how they can help. You are special indeed."

Lucy's face noticeably brightened at his words as her mom introduced herself and asked if there was anything they could do to assist. "Thank you," Charlie said, "but I'm okay for the moment. You have already done more than enough. It is nice to meet you both."

And with that, they said their goodbyes and were on their way. But the story doesn't end there.

You see, Lucy was intent on helping those who, unlike her, didn't have a home. So she began hitting up her family members for cash. "I'm raising money for the homeless!" she would say cheerfully. She even hit up her grandmother, who lived in a nursing home.

A couple days after meeting Charlie, Lucy rolled into the kitchen where her mom was fixing lunch. "Can I have a lemonade stand?" the seven-year-old girl asked.

Within minutes, armed with a pitcher of Crystal Light lemonade, a sleeve of paper cups, and a homemade sign, Lucy was in business.

Flagging down people driving through her neighborhood, Lucy shared how she was raising money for the homeless. She was charging twenty-five cents a cup, but her customers always threw in a little extra since it was for a good cause.

By the end of the day, her impromptu enterprise had added a few dollars to her fund. But she wasn't done. The next day, she enlisted a couple of her friends to join her in going door-to-door in her neighborhood to again raise money for the homeless.

Lucy's mom watched what was occurring with a bit of amazement. After all, no one had suggested she do any fundraising. She did it all on her own—setting a grown-up sized example worth emulating in the process.

Between her family, neighbors and lemonade stand, Lucy raised almost ninety dollars. At first, she wanted to take the whole sum and deliver it to Charlie or another homeless person she found sitting on a bench, but her mom suggested she donate the money to a rescue mission. This way, they could help many people.

Lucy liked the idea, and she and her mom decided to visit the local mission at the end of the week.

The day before the trip, the telephone rang at the Mixson home. It was Miss Maiers, Lucy's second-grade teacher. "I just wanted to let you know that Lucy has written a letter to her classmates saying she is going to the rescue mission tomorrow. If the other kids have any money or clothes they want to donate, she'll be happy to take it when she goes."

Once again, Lucy's mom was astonished. She had thought her daughter's fundraising drive was done. But then, without fanfare, Lucy kept on going. The morning of the mission trip, some of her classmates brought clothes and a few brought money. Miss Maiers even broke a twenty-dollar bill into singles and let every student contribute a dollar.

No one anticipated the chain reaction caused by Lucy's initiative. Her small acts of determined kindness were like stones in a pond, the ripples spreading out to family, friends, neighbors, classmates, and even her teacher. By the day of her trip to the mission, Lucy had raised almost $130 in coins and cash. More importantly, she had taught everyone that leadership isn't something you wait to be thrust upon you. It's something you activate within yourself—seizing the initiative and adding value to your surroundings, one others-centered act at a time.

*   *   *

We can all learn from Lucy's positive example by applying her brand of leadership to our surroundings. If you're unsure how to get started, try one of these suggestions:

Take time to meet someone new. Most people have a habit of stagnating in a small circle of friends; but doing so limits our ability to grow. Do as Lucy did and step out of your comfort zone. Get out there and meet new people. You'll be surprised at the lessons that each person can teach you and the new energy and enthusiasm they can infuse into your life.

Smile. A smile is the fastest way to set positive change into motion. It can turn the most awkward of moments into an opportunity to ease circumstances for those around you. Scientists tell us that the simple act of smiling sends a message to your brain that you're happy. When you're happy, you increase the likelihood of that same sentiment spreading to those around you.

Treat everyone you meet with kindness and respect. No boundary or class can dictate or take away that right. Make it a habit to treat everyone you meet with the same level of respect that you would give your grandparents, regardless if someone is a self-made millionaire or a homeless veteran. People will notice your thoughtfulness.

Be ready to perform one selfless act every day. In life, you get out what you put in. When you make it a priority to create a positive impact in someone else's life, you enrich your own in the process. Choose to do something today (and every day) that's not about you. I promise you'll never regret it.

I often wonder how much better the world would be if each of us seized even one opportunity daily to emulate seven-year-old Lucy? What if we routinely chose to act on ordinary opportunities to make the world a little better than we found it? I don't know about you, but I'm confident it would be a brighter, kinder world indeed.

Lemonade stand not necessary.

INSPIRE

Others-centered leaders understand motivation can be manufactured but inspiration must be instilled. They recognize that when a leader nurtures a working environment motivated by inspiration, those around them are not afraid to push past their fears in the direction of their dreams.

40

Be Better, Not Bitter

"Let your past make you better, not bitter."
Unknown

Louis (Louie) Zamperini deeply understood the transformative power
of hope to make us better, not bitter.

Zamperini, a former Olympic distance runner, joined the military
in the 1940's so he could do his part to defend freedom and defeat our
nation's enemies. Shortly into his tour of duty in the Pacific, Louie was
shot down in his B-24 bomber, the *Green Hornet*.

For weeks, the survivors of the crash floated, followed by sharks,
surviving on rainwater and the few fish and birds they could catch. On
the twenty-seventh day afloat, a plane appeared. Louie enthusiastically
fired flares, and the plane turned toward them. But the promise of
rescue quickly turned into another struggle for survival as the aircraft
turned out to be a Japanese bomber.

As the enemy plane fired machine guns at the castaways, Louie leaped
overboard. He had to kick and punch the circling sharks to keep them
away until the firing from the enemy plane stopped and he could climb
back up onto the raft. Over and over, the Japanese bomber returned to
strafe the men, sending Louie back into the shark-infested water.

After drifting for an incredible forty-seven days, he was eventually
captured by the very enemy he had set out to fight. For the next two

years, Louie was held in a tiny, filthy cell and was repeatedly starved, beaten, and interrogated. He was eventually transferred to a prison camp in Japan, where he encountered a monstrous guard known as the Bird.

Fixated on breaking the famous former Olympian, the Bird beat Louie relentlessly and forced him to do slave labor. After relentless abuse at the hands of his attacker, Louie reached the end of his endurance. With his dignity destroyed and his will fading, he prayed for rescue.

When the atomic bombs ended hostilities, the Bird fled to escape war crimes trials, and Louie was saved from almost certain death. But he came home a broken, bitter man.

Louie returned to California a national hero. He married a beautiful woman named Cynthia, but even her love couldn't blot out the memories of the nightmare he had experienced at the hand of his captors. He sought solace in running, but an ankle injury, incurred in a POW camp and exacerbated by the Bird's beatings, hampered him. Just as he was reaching Olympic form again, his ankle failed. His athletic career was finished. Weighed down by an almost uncontrollable sense of anger and ever present state of bitterness, Louie was cast into another prison of sorts—this time by alcohol.

For years, Louie struggled. His inability to shed his past hurts or subdue his ever-present fear led him deeper into despair; ultimately, pushing him to the brink of losing everything: His wife, his child, and even his life. Yet, he endured. In fact, he not only survived, but he also went on to subsequently thrive, restoring a broken marriage, building a successful business, and, most importantly, discovering the power of hope, that unseen commodity that brings comfort to our aching souls and brings light into even the darkest moments of our lives.

*   *   *

Hope has been described in many ways. To some, it is the promise of future good. To others, it is the ability to persevere and prevail, no matter how daunting life's storms. Yet, others equate hope to merely a fanciful wish.

In his personal memoir, *Devil at my Heels*, Zamperini attributes his ability to bounce back, to successfully navigate the storms of his life, to a single primary virtue: "...a part of you still believes you can fight and survive no matter what your mind knows. It's not so strange. Where there's still life, there's still *hope*." In other words, hope is a gift to the world, always available for the taking.

To me, hope is an amazing and necessary force for good that points our imagination toward positive things. It's a word that explodes with confidence and compels us to believe in something bigger than ourselves. It is, as Louie Zamperini discovered first hand, an unseen commodity that pays dividends while we still live.

If we are careful to pay attention, we can actually see hope all around us. For example:

> Hope is seen in the sprouting seedling that shoots up from the crevasse of a massive rock.

> Hope is heard in the cry of a newborn baby once tightly bound and now liberated to grow into the fullness of its potential.

> Hope is seen in the promise of a new day by the rising of the morning sun.

> Hope is heard in the voices of those who speak on behalf of the marginalized, the poor, and all those powerless to change their current circumstances.

> Hope is seen in the eyes of addicts who finally kick their habits, in the face of the couple committed to saving their troubled marriage, and in the example of your neighbor who chooses to fight back against a devastating (and potentially deadly) medical diagnosis.

Hope, the promise of future good, is all around us. It is priceless and free for the taking. All we have to do is learn to pay attention.

Hope is the acid test of leadership.

* * *

For decades, the world has marveled at a once crown jewel known as the Hope Diamond. This dazzling, blue, 45-carat gem with an estimated value of $250 million is a truly one-of-a-kind treasure. Its last owner chose to donate the historic treasure to the Smithsonian Museum as "a gift to the world", where, today, it sits encased behind thick bulletproof glass.

The question I have for you is, are you freely sharing the gift of hope with the world or are you, too, keeping it locked up, inaccessible, untouchable, where no one can see it? Are you holding on to past hurts, obsessed by destructive thoughts, and convinced your future is only filled with more disappointment and despair?

Here is the good news. It is never too late to begin building greater hope into our lives and in our surroundings? In fact, here are six daily choices you can begin making to promote hope right where you are:

Choose to think in terms of possibilities and solutions, rather than being paralyzed by a sense of your limitations;

Choose to focus on what you can do rather than what you cannot do;

Choose to invest your time, talent and ideas in areas you can effect rather than spending needless energy on what you cannot control;

Choose to operate from your strengths, while remaining realistic about your shortcomings;

Choose to build on the positive aspects of your life in the present rather than fixating on all you wish were different in the future; and finally,

Choose to be a light instead of a judge; an encourager instead of a worrier, and watch as your positive example inspires those around you to begin to do the same.

My hope for you is that you will discover the same truth Louis Zamperini discovered for himself; namely, that hope is a key that unlocks the heart of a better you. It is an invaluable and amazing treasure designed to be shared. It is a wellspring of strength you can draw on to become better rather than remaining bitter. And the best part of all, it is available, free of charge.

Allow hope to put wings on your performance and discover for yourself how it will heighten your happiness, elevate your effectiveness and make you the kind of leader you want to be and others deserve to see.

41

Make Gratitude Your Natural Advantage

"Feeling gratitude and not expressing it is like
wrapping a present and not giving it."
William Arthur Ward

A friend once shared a simple but profound story about a school in a distant village. Now I'm excited to share it with you.

Far, far away, say half a world away, there was a small, brick school. Atop the school was a bell, which rang promptly at eight o'clock every morning to call the children to class. The boys and girls arrived reluctantly and precisely on the hour, never a minute early, occasionally a little late. The bell would ring again at exactly three o'clock every afternoon, liberating the children to go play. At the first sound of the bell, the children would bolt out the door of the school, never lingering a moment longer.

Except for one.

A particular young girl named Marie came early and stayed late every day. She helped the teacher clean the chalkboard, sort papers and tidy up the room. During class she eagerly participated in the lessons.

One day, when the other children were particularly disruptive and inattentive, the teacher singled out the girl as an example. "Why can't each of you be more like Marie? She listens; she arrives early and stays late."

Almost immediately one of the boys from the back of the room spoke up, blurting out, "It isn't fair to ask us to be like her."

"Why not?" asked the teacher.

The boy squirmed in his chair. It was clear he was uncomfortable answering the question. "Because she has an advantage," he replied.

"And what might that be?"

"She's an orphan," he whispered, almost under his breath.

The young boy was right. Marie was an orphan and she did have an advantage, an advantage of knowing that being at school was better than being at the orphanage. At school she felt she was building toward a better future. At school she knew she could contribute her time and talent to helping others have a better, brighter day.

At school, she was grateful for what others took for granted.

*   *   *

Gratitude has been defined as possessing or experiencing a sense of thankfulness in response to receiving something beneficial. Webster's dictionary describes it as "the quality of feeling or being grateful or thankful." In many ways, it is the ultimate positive emotion as it expands our sense of well-being and enhances our appreciation for those people or things that brighten our day or lighten our load. Perhaps this is why gratitude is frequently described as *a gift that keeps on giving.*

The philosopher Cicero once said, "Gratitude is not only the greatest of virtues but the parent of all the others." Years later, sociologist Georg Simmel referred to gratitude as "the moral memory of mankind ... if every grateful action ... were suddenly eliminated, society (at least as we know it) would break apart."

These insightful words alert us to the power of gratitude to reorient our perspectives, lift our spirits and even improve our lives. As Yale University researcher Shawn Achor shares, "...gratitude is not only one of the fastest ways to raise the level of happiness, it literally transforms your health." Yes, gratitude is a positive force, indeed.

183

Science confirms that guarding ourselves from taking things for granted makes us more willing to accept responsibility for others, less likely to judge the value of others based on their position or possessions, and more conscientious, more agreeable, more compassionate, and less envious and egotistical than non-grateful people. In other words, gratefulness positions us to model humanity operating at its peak, positive capacity.

What's essential to recognize, however, is that although we all have opportunities to express thankfulness, too few of us *choose* to regularly act on those opportunities. We only need to look at the low level of employee engagement in our workplaces, assess the number of discouraged children and spouses in our homes, or examine the lack of mutually beneficial relationships in our communities to see that gratitude, though in abundant supply, is a commodity many fail to frequently share.

Don't let that be you.

British writer G. K. Chesterton is considered by many to be one of the major literary figures of the 20th century. His influence on literature was eclipsed only by his zeal for life. To what was this sense of ever-present exuberance and exhilaration attributed? In a word, it was *gratitude*.

In his autobiography, written just before his passing in 1936, Chesterton summarized his view of gratitude as "if not the doctrine I have always taught, is the doctrine I should have always liked to teach." Today, almost eight decades after he wrote those words, their meaning rings just as insightfully. That is, they remain a testimony to the truth that there exists no lack of opportunities to practice gratefulness in and through our lives, only an absence of commitment. Each of us has immediately within our reach the ability to share a kind word, pen a pleasant note of thanks, or offer someone the gift of our undivided help or attention.

Learn a lesson from Marie, the grateful orphan, and exercise your natural advantage. Choose to take fewer things for granted and you too will discover that every moment is spring loaded with possibilities to make our world a better, brighter place to live, work, and play.

Why wait? Resolve to be more grateful, beginning today. I promise you won't regret it.

42

Pursue the Road Less Traveled

"Knowledge will give you power, but character respect."
Bruce Lee

Anyone who thinks about September 11, 2001 will likely remember exactly where they were when they heard the news on that fateful fall morning. It is an event forever seared into our collective national and global consciousness – a date that marks the end of one era and the start of another.

Within minutes of the attacks on New York City, news stations began reporting events, while numerous federal, state, and local agencies struggled to not only better understand what was happening but also try to predict what might happen next.

Across the nation, the Federal Aviation Administration, the agency responsible for managing airspace and airports across America, frantically sought to positively identify the hundreds of aircraft still airborne, intent on determining if any further hijacked aircraft existed.

Just minutes into their assessment, they learned of a third aircraft careening into the Pentagon. Shortly thereafter, they identified a fourth aircraft, United Flight 93, had also deviated from its flight plan and was no longer responding to controller's queries.

In the midst of all these near-simultaneous events, our nation's military went to its highest state of alert, immediately launching numerous armed interceptor jet aircraft to engage and, if need be, eliminate any confirmed threats to American lives.

It was truly a dynamic, fast-paced, tension-filled time.

Shortly after the third plane careened into the Pentagon, a key military command center in Alaska, working closely with local FAA controllers, began tracking a commercial passenger jet inbound to Alaska that would not respond to radio transmissions. Seconds turned into minutes and it quickly became apparent an intercept and possible engagement was imminent.

It was an engagement that could result in the loss of yet more American lives.

Suddenly, a terrible situation had gone from bad to worse and the unthinkable instantly became all-too-plausible.

Aircraft from the United States Air forces Third Fighter Wing in Alaska were immediately launched, setting out to intercept this mysterious jet. It was quickly identified as a large passenger airliner much like those used in the east coast attacks. It, too, was not responding to repeated attempts to establish radio communication. The very real potential that one of our nation's fighter aircraft may be called upon to "engage" a civilian passenger airliner was becoming more real by the second.

If this were to occur, it would be the first-ever such engagement in our nation's history, one that would result in the willful sacrifice of civilian lives in the air to protect an untold number of others on the ground.

Thus, with time working against them, a crisis was mounting in the military command center in Alaska.

Leader of Sound Character

Because of the dynamic nature of the situation, there was very little time to fully comprehend the full extent of the decisions and subsequent ramification that may very likely have to be made in this rapidly-unfolding situation.

However, it was precisely at this critical moment that the leader of the organization, Lieutenant General Norton "Norty" Schwartz, then Commander of the Alaskan Command and Eleventh Air Force, made a crucial choice. Realizing that circumstances had placed his organization in unchartered territory and that any decision he made could potentially put anyone in the command center at risk of criminal prosecution or a civil suit, he chose to direct everyone present to leave.

All, that is, but a single controller who was needed to maintain communication with the FAA.

In this moment of great uncertainty, General Schwartz clearly realized the bearing his actions would have on everyone involved. Although the safest choice may well have been to wait for someone higher up in the chain of command to make the call, he recognized the window for action was rapidly closing. So instead of deferring his decision, he chose to own it, potential consequences and all.

Working through the lone controller to personally guide the interceptor aircraft toward the airliner, General Schwartz prepared to do what he must to protect our country from further attack. Fortunately, moments before he had to make the dreadful decision, FAA controllers were able to regain communications with the aircraft and direct it to a nearby airport. It soon landed without incident, escorted by several of our nation's most lethal jet aircraft.

In these tension-filled moments, General Schwartz proved himself to be a leader unafraid to accept responsibility for his decisions. He demonstrated by his attitudes and actions that he was a leader of unshakeable character committed to pursuing the path less traveled despite the potential cost to self.

Needed: Façade Free Leadership

In the past, the development of character was a national priority. Our social structures, families, neighborhoods, schools, and communities could be counted on to provide safety, support, and civility. We once made it a national priority to learn about our nation's forefathers and the heroic men and women who selflessly invested their lives in pursuing noble ends for the benefit of the greater good.

Today, much has changed.

We live and operate in a society where character is often crowded out by convenience. Leaders willing to do what is right, regardless of the potential cost to self, have become an all too rare commodity.

Think of the many well-known leaders who have chosen to amass fortunes at the expense of those who count on them to have their best interest at heart: Ken Lay of Enron, Dennis Kozlowski of Tyco, and Bernie Ebbers of WorldCom. Each of these men led organizations that intentionally misled their employees and shareholders. Instead of being driven by a desire to strive to do great things for others, they succumbed to gathering and hoarding more for themselves. In other words, their lack of character perpetuated a façade, which, once revealed, resulted in millions of people losing their paychecks and pensions, forever.

Character forms the foundation of effective leadership. When people in positions of authority and responsibility act in unscrupulous ways, trust plummets. Yet when a leader consistently stands on principle, especially when it is personally or professionally inconvenient or unpopular to do so, confidence soars. As I bring this chapter to a close, let me leave you with a final story from Greek mythology to further illuminate my point.

As a young man, the Greek hero Hercules once came to a fork in the road where two women stood. One woman, named Pleasure, told him that her road was sweet, pleasant, and carefree, and would lead him through a gentle valley of flowery meadows, where he would experience no stress or strain. The other woman, Virtue, pointed to her road, which looked steep, rocky, and led toward a very steep mountain. She said she could promise him nothing but what his own sweat, toil, labor, and strength would produce. Hercules chose the latter, more challenging road, which turned out to be the path toward the true heights of greatness.

My question for you is, which road will you pick the next time you're faced with the choice to live up and into your character? Will you go the way of self-promotion, self-service, or pleasure and do what's easy, safe, and personally or professionally convenient? Or, will you do as General Schwartz did on September 11, 2001, and risk doing what must be done to support the greater good, despite the potential cost to self - willingly owning tough decisions, potential consequences, and all?

43

Become a More Effective & Empathetic You

*"The last of the human freedoms is
to choose one's attitudes."*
Victor Frankl

Viktor Frankl was an incredible person by many measures. He was a brilliant academic, a survivor of the Holocaust, a pioneering neurologist and psychiatrist in Vienna following World War II, and an inspirational author. Most notable, however, is that his finest moments came when leadership was thrust upon him in the bleakest of times.

Despite enduring the atrocities of four Nazi concentration camps, the most infamous being Auschwitz, and losing his wife and parents to them, Frankl managed to find what few others could during such a dark period in our world's history: a meaningful purpose for living. Instead of allowing the despairing conditions he found himself in to overwhelm or engulf him, Frankl chose to transform his circumstances into an opportunity to grow in ways he didn't think possible. How? By resisting the tendency to turn inward and become paralyzed by fear, resentment, anger, and self-pity. Despite facing incredibly challenging circumstances, he chose to willfully orient outward and discover what he could do to help lighten the load, lift the spirits and selflessly serve those around him.

After the war, Frankl recounted his varied trials, tribulations, and professional experiences in a series of books that continue to be counted among the most influential of our time. In fact, his writings are largely regarded as masterpieces for their ability to paint images of seemingly average individuals, whose empathy for the plight of others challenges each of us to re-think our notions of what constitutes an extraordinary person or a truly successful leader.

Finding Meaning through Service

Perhaps the most significant aspect of Frankl's personal transformation from concentration camp victim to purposeful leader, occurred as a result of what he saw transpiring in the daily events of the Nazi death camps. These were situations which, over time, taught him firsthand how one of the most important things a leader can do for those in their care is to learn to see events through another's eyes or walk a mile in their shoes.

In his inspirational memoir, *Man's Search for Meaning*, Frankl recounts how, over time, he became transfixed at the sight of others willfully ignoring their own hardships in order to reach out in service to those who needed their help the most. In one account, he recalls a particularly cold morning when he and other prisoners were forced to stumble in the darkness over big stones and through large puddles along the one road leading from the camp. The guards were shouting at the prisoners, driving them forward with the butts of their rifles. The only way some of these prisoners were able to make it was by supporting themselves on their neighbor's arm. Hardly a word was spoken; the icy wind did not encourage talk. But the prisoners' concern for one another was readily expressed in their selfless actions and provided the physical and emotional strength necessary to overcome the cruelty they collectively faced.

Little by little, in the midst of one of our world's darkest moments, Frankl discovered the transformative ability of selflessness to overpower selfishness. It was a discovery that even today serves to remind those of us wanting to become better leaders how developing a great sense of caring for all people, foes as well as friends alike, requires that we learn to routinely look beyond ourselves by making empathy an indispensable part of our lives.

Choosing to See Beyond Ourselves

In his international bestseller *The Courageous Follower*, Ira Chaleff says that, as leaders, "we can model any characteristic we possess or develop, but the most important one to model may be empathy."

In simplest terms, empathy is the ability to put oneself in another's shoes. Or, in the words of psychiatrist Alfred Adler, empathy is "to see with the eyes of another, to hear with the ears of another, and to feel with the heart of another." Unlike sympathy, where you choose to remain an outsider content with viewing the situation from a distance, empathy actively involves the observer. There is an intentional emotional connection made with the other person as you make the choice to better understand what they are seeing, feeling, or experiencing.

But why does the importance of empathy still seem so hard to accept? Is it a practice that is only well suited for our homes or worship spaces but inappropriate for our workplaces?

Sadly, I believe that this remains a common misconception.

Admittedly, empathy seems to have little place in the traditional top-down model of leadership, perhaps because choosing to see events through another's eyes or walk a mile in their shoes smacks of weakness. It sounds soft and mushy and doesn't resonate well with the vigorous phrases we often associate with leadership.

Words such as vision and daring, conviction and courage, assertiveness and integrity naturally come to mind. Empathy doesn't often make the leadership cut. But empathy, seeing with the eyes of another, hearing with the ears of another, and feeling with the heart of another, demonstrates our capacity and willingness to project ourselves into the position of another.

The truth is, empathy, being open to understanding the perspectives, emotions, thoughts, concerns, and motives of others, is not about embracing blind agreement in order to please those around you. Rather, it's about being open to better understanding others and working to gain an increased appreciation for their circumstances.

Recognizing Everyone Has Value

One of my favorite examples of the importance of learning to appreciate the innate value and worth of every person we encounter comes from a true story from a 1996 edition of *Guideposts*. To this day it is a piece I reread periodically to remind me of the importance of practicing empathy in our lives:

"During my second month of nursing school, our professor gave us a pop quiz. I was a conscientious student and breezed through the questions, until I read the last one: 'What is the first name of the woman who cleans the school?'"

"Surely, this was some kind of joke. I had seen the cleaning woman several times. She was tall, dark-haired, and in her fifties, but how would I know her name? I handed in my paper, leaving the last question blank."

"Before the class ended, one student asked if the last question would count toward the quiz grade. 'Absolutely,' said the professor. 'In your careers you will meet many people. All are significant. They deserve your attention and care.'"

"I've never forgotten that lesson. I also learned her name was Dorothy."

As this simple but powerful example affirms, empathy empowers you to build and develop genuine appreciation for those around you; it enables you to gain a greater awareness of the needs of those around you, and it encourages you to create an environment of open communication and more effective feedback so others feel safe enough to be who they really are around you.

As you seek to become a more effective and empathetic leader, here are three practical strategies you can apply in your own sphere of influence to create conditions for trust, transparency, collaboration and mutual appreciation to flourish around you:

Cultivate Curiosity: Empathic people have an insatiable curiosity about strangers. They possess a natural inquisitiveness that makes them comfortable reaching out to others around them. Be it talking to someone you don't know on a bus, spending time with an old acquaintance on the phone, or taking time to inquire into the interests of the barista at the local coffee shop, challenge yourself to learn something new and novel about those around you at least once every day. Make a commitment to become a respectful inquirer. Cultivate curiosity wherever you go and you will likely be pleasantly surprised by what you discover.

Seek Commonalities: We all make assumptions about others and use collective labels that create barriers to our appreciating the uniqueness and individuality of others. Challenge yourself to suspend your preconceptions and prejudices and search for what you may have in common with others. Focus on all the things you could learn from someone different than you rather than fixating on all the reasons why they are different from you. In the wise words of actor Harrison Ford, "What's important is to be able to see yourself...as having commonality with other people and not determine...that everybody is less significant, less interesting, less important than you are."

Invest in Meaningful Relationships: If the 20th century was the Age of Introspection, when self-help and therapy culture encouraged us to look inside ourselves to try and find true satisfaction and happiness, then the 21st century is proving to be the Age of *otherliness*. That is, it affirms how leading a life of purpose, meaning, and significance isn't merely a matter of intense self-reflection. Instead, it is being genuinely interested in the lives of others. Bill Drayton, the renowned "father of social entrepreneurship," believes that in the era of rapid technological change in which we find ourselves today, mastering empathy is an essential survival skill as it underpins successful teamwork and leadership.

Of the many important lessons we can learn from Victor Frankl's time in the concentration camps, perhaps the greatest is that, no matter how daunting our circumstances, situations or surroundings, when we choose to be generous with others when we don't have to be, show kindness and act with compassion with others when it's not easy, and give freely of ourselves for the benefit of another when doing the minimum is all others expect to see, nothing becomes impossible. Internalizing this simple but potentially transformative truth can do wonders for our effectiveness as leaders. It also helps us better understand what Frankl truly meant when he wrote, "We who lived in concentration camps can remember the men who walked through the huts comforting others, giving away their last piece of bread. They may have been few in number, but they offer sufficient proof that everything can be taken from a man but one thing: the last of human freedoms - to choose one's attitude in any given set of circumstances - to choose one's own way."

How are you choosing, today?

44

Follow Well First

"Leaders rarely use their power wisely or effectively over long periods unless they are supported by followers who have the stature to help them do so."
Ira Chaleff

One of the long standing traditions associated with beginning a New Year is to resolve to do something different in the future. To some of us, that different something may mean committing to exercise more, eat healthier, learn a new skill, eliminate a bad habit, and the list of possibilities goes on and on. This year, I've chosen a very different resolution than I have in the past. Instead of striving to run a marathon, pen a book proposal, or learn to paint, I've committed to doing something really, really challenging (for me, anyway).

I've decided I need to work on becoming a better follower.

You see, for as long as I can remember, I've been working on becoming a successful leader. I've read scores of books, attended countless leadership development programs at prestigious schools, and, most importantly, have been privileged to exercise leadership in both peace and war. But for the thousands of hours I've invested in trying to become a better boss, I've spent very few working through what it means to become a successful follower.

It shouldn't be a surprise to anyone reading this that we are a society seemingly infatuated with leadership and disinterested in followership. Though the subjects are inseparable, we certainly don't seem to value followership the same way we lionize leadership. In fact, if we are honest with ourselves, it is certainly easy to understand why most people prefer to be a leader—*following* just doesn't feel as important as *leading*.

The fact of the matter is, nothing could be further from the truth. You see, I've come to understand that true success isn't a function of one particular person's special skills but rather, it is a byproduct of the contribution of people all the way up and down the organizational chart. In fact, research confirms leaders contribute on the average no more than 20% to the success of organizations. It's the followers who are critical to the completion of the remaining 80%.

Given that leadership and followership are so inextricably linked, how can you go about transforming the nature of your relationship with your boss? How can you ensure you are doing your part to be an effective follower? The answer is found in a single, unlikely, if not admittedly uncomfortable, word: *Submit.*

To submit is to surrender (oneself) to the will or authority of another person. Derived from ancient Greek military imagery, the word literally refers to those who were "ranked under" someone in an established position of power. Submission then speaks to our willingly serving and supporting those placed in positions over us. by choosing how we can best translate desired intentions into meaningful actions.

Let's be clear. Submission is not natural nor is it something that is particularly popular. Signing up to support someone else's agenda, promote someone else's plan, and follow someone else's direction isn't easy, but it is necessary if you are committed to standing up and for your leader.

So what can you begin doing to invest more time in becoming a better follower? I recommend you start by keeping this mnemonic, SUBMIT, in mind:

Silence your Inner Critic. It is easier to criticize than it is to empathize. If you are honest with yourself, there is virtually no instance when you will fully understand why your boss is asking what they are asking or directing what they are directing. To become a better follower, you have to trust there is more at play than you see. Assist your boss in becoming a better leader by asking respectful questions or sharing information they may not have. Help him or her do a better job by silencing your inner critic. Choose to be helpful instead of disrespectful.

Understand Your Own Limitations. One of the keys to becoming a better follower is being real about what you can and cannot control. When bringing an issue to your boss for a decision, do your homework and have as much relevant information as possible. Know the pros and the cons, the upside and the potential downside. Don't take it personally when your ideas are challenged or your opinion disregarded. Remember, it is your job to provide your boss the best possible information and advice you can muster. It is your boss's responsibility to decide if he or she will put it to good use.

Be a Problem Solver, Not a Problem Spotter. No one likes being around someone who is quick to bemoan all that is wrong, yet never seems to offer ideas on how to make them right. Bosses innately appreciate followers who illuminate challenges and then do the extra work to identify solutions to address these problems. So the next time you are inclined to communicate an issue or shortcoming, be sure you finish the thought. Commit to solving problems instead of merely spotting them.

Make Time to Get Out of Your Head and into Your Heart. One of the most frustrating things for a leader is to assign a task or give an order and then watch the ball drop because the person didn't follow through on what they said they would do. Effective followers give their best effort toward completing the work assigned to them, knowing the outcome reflects not only their reputations, but also those of the leader and the entire team. Giving your best, especially when frustration and stress levels are high, won't happen with half-hearted devotion.

Insist On Managing Your Emotions. Emotion can quickly get the best of us, especially if we are passionate about a subject or convinced of the validity of our position. There will be days when your boss may seem unreasonable, but you must remember they are the ones accountable for results. Rather than push back on their position in public, ask to discuss your concerns with him or her in private. Chances are, the better you are at keeping your emotions in check, the greater your likelihood of influencing your boss to take your opinion, idea, or concern seriously. Let your objectivity create a cycle of mutual receptivity.

Tell Yourself Regularly, If It is to be, It Must Begin with Me. You may not always agree with the manner in which your boss chooses to lead and that's okay. We all possess skills others don't. To be a good follower means you willingly come alongside your boss to make the team better, bringing insights, talents, and resources they can't produce without you. As author Ira Chaleff reminds us, "At the heart of all transformation of relationships lies transformation of ourselves." Never forget, the most powerful tool you have to promote positive change is setting a good example. Be the leader you want to see by committing to being the best follower you can be.

With all this in mind, perhaps we shouldn't be surprised to discover a popular definition of followership simply reads *"a position of submission to a leader."* That's it. No long list of traits provided. No complicated formula or elaborate description required. Seven words that tell us everything we need to know: To follow, we need to accept a particular position (submission) in support of a particular person (your boss), making what is important to them important to you...understanding the best investments you can make in becoming a better leader is learning to truly appreciate what it takes to be a successful follower.

45

Lead with Love

"There's nobody I know who commands the love of others who doesn't feel like a success. And I can't imagine people who aren't loved feel very successful."
Warren Buffett

There is a legend that tells how, many years ago in Scotland, a large eagle snatched a sleeping baby from the front of a small cottage. Numerous people witnessed the event, and they quickly gathered the entire village to rescue the infant. However, eagles fly and people don't. So, it escaped, landing in a lofty crag high in the mountains above the village.

Almost immediately, many gave up hope that the child could be recovered. Nonetheless, several villagers chose to exhaust all possible opportunities to save the baby.

The magnitude of the challenge before them was overshadowed only by the courage and commitment that swelled within them.

The first person to attempt a rescue was a brave sailor who had only recently returned from the sea. He set out with fierce determination, scaling the mountain hand over hand. But in time, he reached an impassable obstacle, acknowledged defeat, and abandoned the effort.

Though he possessed the courage to try, his commitment to the cause was derailed by the magnitude of the challenge before him.

Next, a rugged and experienced highlander stepped up to the challenge. He was a strong man with many years of mountain climbing experience. He set out with great determination and, although he made it a little further than the sailor, he could not quite make it to the top either. Exhausted, his enthusiasm depleted, he turned back, his objective unattained.

Finally, the only person left was a meek, middle-aged peasant woman who stood by silently watching all that was going on. Then, quite unexpectedly, she too set out to try to save the baby. No one said anything, but it was obvious that everyone was thinking if a healthy, young sailor and a rugged highlander had failed to scale the heights, what chance did this meek woman have?

Though they admired her commitment, they doubted her potential.

The peasant woman quietly removed her shoes and started forward, carefully placing one bare foot in front of the other along the shelf of the cliff. Slowly, she rose higher and higher until, much to everyone's surprise, she reached the child. She tenderly lifted the baby from the eagle's nest while the villagers waiting below watched anxiously and fearfully.

The descent from the mountain was in many ways more difficult than the ascent. One wrong step would certainly result in death for both the peasant woman and the child. But, slowly, the woman descended, careful of her every movement. As she took the final step down the mountain the villagers rushed forward to welcome her, still incredulous at her feat and profoundly moved by both her courage and commitment.

Many started asking how she was able to muster the strength and determination to achieve something so difficult, something so risky. They wondered aloud how she, against all odds, was able to succeed where others, seemingly more capable, had failed.

The peasant woman looked at those gathered around her and said: "It was simple. This is my daughter. As a mother, my love for her motivated me to scale heights the others could only dream about. My hope for her future inspired me to move forward when I was tempted to turn back. My unconditional commitment to her gave me the courage to continue even when the path ahead was uncertain."

* * *

For ages, scholars have defined love as the power that joins and binds the universe and everything in it. Love is considered the great harmonizing principle and, in the words of philosopher and theologian Teilhard de Chardin, love is the "only force that can make things one without destroying them." Only love has the power to transform lives, heal sickness, mute evil, and reap harmony from discord.

Yes, I am convinced; love is indeed one of the most incredibly powerful forces available to mankind.

Who reading this has not heard of the power of love to spawn one of mythologies greatest tales, the Trojan War? This was a war that raged for 10 years and cost scores of lives, destroyed thousands of ships, and marked the end of many of the greatest heroes of the age. Again, this happened all in the name of love. Or, who has not been moved by great movies such as *Gone with the Wind*, a brilliant and captivating tale of the power of love set in the midst of our nation's Civil War? Or what of the many great scholars and poets who have tried for generations to capture the essence of the transformative power of love to bring about change and healing in a world constantly beset by travails?

Here is the great news. Leading with love doesn't have to be relegated to timeless legends, famous myths, or fabulous novels. You can demonstrate your commitment to creating conditions for those around you to flourish and thrive by keeping these four imperatives in mind:

> **Be Inclusive**: Listen to other people's ideas, no matter how different they may be from your own. There's ample evidence that the most imaginative and valuable ideas tend not to come from the top of an organization, but from within an organization. Be inclusive and open yourself to the opinions of

others; what you hear may make the difference between merely being good and ultimately becoming great.

Be Inquisitive: Ask great questions. The most effective leaders know they don't have all the answers. Instead, they constantly welcome and seek out new knowledge and insist on tapping into the curiosity and imaginations of those around them. Take it from Albert Einstein: "I have no special talent," he claimed. "I am only passionately curious." Be inquisitive. Help tap others' hidden genius, one wise question and courageous conversation at a time.

Be Intentional: Don't fall prey to your own publicity: Spin and sensationalism is an attractive angle to take in today's self-promoting society. Yet, the more we become accustomed to seeking affirmation or basking in the glow of others' praise and adulation, the more it dilutes our objectivity, diminishes our focus, and sets us up to believe others are put in our path to serve our needs. Be intentional in being hopeful and helpful, but be careful not to become prideful; it will only set you up for a fall.

Be Selfless. Embrace and promote a spirit of selfless service. People, be they employees, customers, constituents, or colleagues, are quick to figure out which leaders are truly dedicated to helping them succeed and which are only interested in promoting themselves at the expense of others. Be willing to put others' legitimate needs and desires first and trust that they will freely give you the best they have to give. Be selfless by committing to lead yourself well. Others will be inspired by your positive example.

Leading with love, then, is what keeps us moving forward toward achieving our greatest, positive potential as a person. It's what helps us grow from both the joyful and the painful circumstances encountered in this journey called life. It's what allows us to muster the personal power not to give up, even when circumstances would try and convince us to do otherwise. Powerful enough, in fact, to help us, as it did the peasant woman, to scale new heights and reach peaks others can only dream of attaining.

46

Choose to Pursue Your Heart's Desire

"If you want to know how to have the life you desire, follow your heart today."
Eric Wahl

Long before Dorothy and Toto ever showed up on the scene in the classic film *The Wizard of Oz*, the Tin Man had a story each of us should hear.

Once a human lumberjack, the Tin Man lived in the munchkin village and fell madly in love with a beautiful munchkin girl. Their situation was complicated by the inconvenient fact that the munchkin beauty was a slave to the Wicked Witch of the East. A careful analysis of munchkin history reveals that the wicked witch eventually grew fearful that the lumberjack would take the munchkin slave away, so she chose to put a curse on the lumberjack's ax. Each time he went to chop a piece of wood, the ax would slip and instead cut off a part of his body.

Undeterred in his love for the beautiful munchkin girl, the lumberjack kept chopping and his body parts kept disappearing. Piece by piece, his body fell apart and, eventually, the only way he could carry on his duties was to allow the tinsmith in the village to replace his severed parts with artificial limbs made of tin.

In time, the once human lumberjack was made entirely of tin—even his heart. The only way he could continue to function properly was to regularly use his oilcan to keep from stiffening and rusting. The larger problem, however, was that he recognized his tin heart could no longer love the munchkin beauty the way he once had. So instead of abandoning his love for her, he chose to set out on a journey to find a new heart, intent in the process to rediscover the man he had once been and rekindle the love he and his munchkin beauty once shared.

So what does this prelude to *the Wizard of Oz* have to do with you, you ask? Simple. This story is a parable that describes the importance of taking a risk to make the necessary changes in your life so you can rediscover what really makes you tick. Consider it a challenge designed to encourage you to exercise the courage of the tin man and face the proverbial wicked witches in your own life—a choice to pursue a path that reunites you with the deepest desires of your heart.

*   *   *

The willingness to change remains one of humanity's oldest dilemmas and, as such, has given birth to the major sciences whose texts now fill the world's libraries. Business managers seek to harness the power of change to maximize value for their shareholders. Marketers seek to understand what prompts one to change from Coke to Pepsi, Nike to Reebok. Psychiatrists and psychologists have developed thousands upon thousands of theories on what practices, therapies, and remedies can best help people navigate change and achieve new levels of wholeness and happiness.

Yet, any way you look at it, change, and the uncertainty that accompanies change, is uncomfortable, unpleasant, and often downright unwelcome for one primary reason: it invokes fear in us. When our hearts and minds are full of fear, science confirms that our natural human response is to do everything we can to reduce if not eliminate outright the source of discomfort we're experiencing in our current circumstances.

Researchers who specialize in studying the brain confirm that, since our arrival on the planet, fear has been an essential tool to protect and preserve human life. As such, it should be no surprise that these same cognitive scientists have also discovered our brains are actually hardwired to *fear first* and *think second*, to maximize our ability to adapt and survive in an ever-changing world. This helps to explain why by the time we begin to experience fear *physiologically*, be it sweaty palms, trembling hands, or a racing heart, our bodies are already hard at work trying to keep us safe by automatically setting into motion our flight or fight response.

What this unconscious response reveals to us then is that our *initial resistance to change is actually a primal instinct*, a natural byproduct of how we are *neurologically* wired as human beings. The bigger problem arises, however, when fear begins to work against us by allowing our unfounded or unexamined concerns of the future to dominate our thinking and drive our decisions. When this occurs, the *psychological* side of fear kicks in to convince us *not* to break our old routines or stretch outside our comfort zones, leaving us instead to abandon the deepest desires of our hearts and settle for leading a life far smaller and narrower than we were ever designed to live.

So though I will be the first to admit that facing the need to change is certainly challenging, I can also confirm resolving to lean into our fear serves another, more empowering purpose. Namely, it prompts us to act. It motivates us to follow the example of the Tin Man and risk pushing off into uncomfortable territory. In other words, facing our fear of change is what helps us grow. It's what reveals all we are capable of being and doing if we allow our dreams to guide us, our imaginations to embolden us and our hearts to lead us.

So what can we as leaders do to help those around us become more comfortable dealing with change? It turns out, just show up. Yup. One of the most effective tools we possess to help others gain the courage to face their fears and the confidence to try new things is to MENTOR them along their journey. Here are some considerations on how to be an effective mentor:

Map others' strengths: Too few leaders take the time to assess individual strengths to be sure that each person is properly aligned with a position that fits them best. If you have ever had to work with someone who is cast in a role that just does not fit them, then you likely know firsthand the resulting loss of productivity, drop in morale, and sagging satisfaction that ensues. Make it a priority to map the strengths of those on your team and you will find people become more comfortable and less anxious of undertaking daunting new challenges.

Enlist your team: For fast-paced, focused leaders, this does not come naturally. This is simply because you are focused on reaching goals and objectives, and having to "slow down" and involve others can make you feel as though you are falling behind schedule. Don't fall into this trap. An excellent way to help others become more comfortable with change is to actively involve them the process early rather than thrusting change upon them months down the line. Share your vision—what you see, where you intend to go—and gather people's input. Invite them to ask questions and provide feedback. Giving those around you a voice in navigating your collective journey helps create buy-in. Come to appreciate that, when asking people to join you in setting off in a new direction, going slow in the beginning in order to enlist others in the cause at hand will ultimately accelerate the rate of progress for everyone.

Notice the good: People crave feedback but they dread the once-a-year review. In many organizations, the annual review is merely a necessary formality. It is something that is done to fill a square and ensure compliance with corporate policy. In fact, research confirms less than a third of companies conduct performance reviews employees deem value-added. So while the annual performance review is often required, choose to do the optional: notice the good things your team members do throughout the year by providing ongoing performance feedback. Nothing beats real-time, on the spot, honest feedback.

Take opportunities to coach: Just as you should be making it a point to notice the good in your team's work, you should also be quick to recognize and remediate issues. After all, as a leader you are also a teacher as well as a coach. Make it a priority to help those around you learn from the various circumstances they encounter by coaching them through the process. Be an enabler of their growth vice merely a judge of their performance. Take a coaching approach (encouraging strong performance and supporting team members after weak performance) will only strengthen your relationships, accelerate your growth, enhance the lives of those around you, and lead to better results.

Open yourself to new learning: Anyone who feels stagnant in their current position will not make a good mentor. People want to feel that the time and energy they spend learning will be rewarded and will ultimately provide them with career satisfaction. Good mentors are committed and are open to experimenting and learning practices that are new to the field. They are excited to share their knowledge with others, understanding the more opportunities and experiences people are exposed to, the more open they become to change. Be a leader who sets the right example by making learning a lifelong endeavour.

Recognize your important role: Great mentors are rare. They're like guardian angels. If you've seen the movie *It's a Wonderful Life*, you know the story of Clarence, the guardian angel. His mission was to help George Bailey through a difficult period. Clarence listened attentively, comforted earnestly, and offered honest advice to George, who initially didn't want to hear it. But eventually, George realized Clarence had his best interest at heart and heeded the advice of his celestial guide—changing his life for the better, as a result.

If you've been leading for any number of years, you know there is one constant: change. Be sure to provide others with opportunities to try new things, provide honest feedback on their performance, and give them access to personal and professional development as it pertains to their positions. This is the heart of mentoring and it is how those around you learn and grow into their full, positive potential.

No yellow brick road required.

47

Be a Leader Others Can Count On

"A man's integrity is his greatest asset –
without integrity you have nothing."
Louis R. Rocco
Recipient of the Congressional Medal of Honor

In 1989, an earthquake in Armenia flattened the entire nation and killed over thirty thousand people in under four minutes. Moments after the ground quit shaking, a father raced to an elementary school to save his son. When he arrived, he saw that the school was gone. It had been reduced to a pile of rubble. Then he remembered a promise he had made to his child, "No matter what happens, you can count on me to be there for you."

Driven by his promise, the father located the approximate area where his son's classroom had once been and started sorting through the debris. Pulling back rocks and clawing through earth, he put all his strength into the monumental effort before him. Soon, other parents arrived and started crying out for their own children. "It's too late," many told the man. "They're all dead. There's nothing you can do to help." But the father didn't stop digging; he just looked at his neighbor and said, "Are you going to help me now?"

Later, the fire chief came and told the man he had to stop, there was no one left alive and he was putting himself in danger. Again, the father simply asked, "Are you going to help me now?" After many more hours of digging, the chief of police came and told him he was putting other people in danger, and ordered him to go home and leave it to the professionals. The man again said nothing but, "Are you going to help me now?"

The father refused to give up. For eight hours, then sixteen, then thirty-six long hours he dug and dug. He dug until his hands were bleeding and muscles aching, but he still refused to quit. Finally, after thirty-eight hours, he pulled aside a large rock and heard the faint whisperings of his son's voice. He called his boy's name, "Arman, Arman!" and out of the darkness a voice answered him, "Dad, it's me!" Then the boy added these priceless words, "I told the other kids not to worry. I told them if you were still alive you'd save me, and when you saved me, they'd be saved, too. Because you promised, 'No matter what happens, you can count on me to be there for you.'"

The lesson for all of us in this story is simple: although we cannot dictate many of the occurrences of our lives, such as when and where we are born or which hardships and trials we'll encounter, we do get to choose if we will keep our promises -to lead a life of unshakable integrity—revealing ourselves to be someone unafraid to do what's right, even if it means we have to go the rest of the journey alone.

*   *   *

Centuries ago, Aristotle pointed out to his pupils how consistently doing right actions forms our identity—integrating what we habitually choose to do into our character. Today, we use the word *integrity* to describe the behavior of those persons who consistently choose to do the right thing, even when doing so is tremendously difficult. That is, we view persons of integrity as individuals whose internal convictions and external actions are so well aligned, so congruent, that they do not stray from what they believe is important even when it may be expedient or personally advantageous to do so.

As leaders, this practice of integrating what we say with what we do is important for many reasons, not the least of which is building trusting relationships. However, many of us know people who have been hurt by those they trusted most and those who have gone back on their word, claiming to say or do something they didn't.

Or we've felt the sting of broken promises ourselves; from parents—ballgames missed, trips never taken; from spouses—marriage vows abandoned; from bosses—opportunities that never materialized.

Failing to make good on our promises is a credibility killer. It diminishes our influence, erodes confidence in our potential, and leaves people questioning whether or not we are, in fact, someone others can really count on.

So please remember, to have integrity is to be integrated, to be whole, to have it all together and, above all, to be consistent in our words and our ways. It's an expressed commitment not to live one life in private and another in public but, rather, to possess the strength of character to withstand the temptation to take the path of least resistance so we can ensure we will be their when others need us most.

48

Be an Inspiration

"First say to yourself what you would be;
and then do what you have to do."
Epictetus

Picture the scene: In a remote part of Afghanistan, near the mountainous border with Pakistan, helicopters carrying dozens of elite Army Rangers race over the rugged landscape. Their target on this high-risk mission is an insurgent compound. It's broad daylight and the Rangers know the insurgents are heavily armed. But it's considered a risk worth taking as reliable intelligence sources indicate a top al Qaeda commander is in that compound.

Within a matter of minutes, the helicopters touch down and the Rangers immediately come under fire. One of the American soldiers who emerged from the helicopter that day was Staff Sergeant Leroy Petry. Seeking cover, Petry and another soldier pushed headlong into courtyard with high mud walls. And that's when the enemy opened up with their AK-47 assault guns.

Leroy is hit in both legs. He's bleeding badly, but he summons the strength to lead the other Ranger to cover. He radios for support while simultaneously hurling a grenade at the enemy, providing cover to a third Ranger who rushes to their aid. Suddenly, an enemy grenade explodes nearby, wounding Leroy's two comrades. And then a second grenade lands -- this time, only a few feet away.

At this point every human impulse would tell a person to turn and run away. After all, every soldier is trained to seek cover. That's what Sergeant Leroy Petry could have done. Instead, this 28-year-old man with his whole life ahead of him, this husband and father of four, did something extraordinary. He lunged forward, toward the live grenade. He picked it up, cocked his arm to throw it back at the enemy, and it exploded, just as it left his hand.

With that selfless act, Leroy saved his two Ranger brothers. But his valor came with a price. The force of the blast took Leroy's right hand. Shrapnel riddled his body. Said one of his teammates later said, "I had never seen someone hurt so bad." Even his combat-tested, battle hardened fellow Rangers were amazed at what Leroy did next. Despite his grievous wounds, he remained calm, actually put on his own tourniquet. He then continued to lead, directing his team, giving orders — even directing the medics how to treat his wounds.

When the fight was over and victory achieved, Leroy lay quietly in a stretcher as he was loaded into a helicopter. Before the helicopter lifted off, one of his teammates ran over to shake Leroy's only remaining hand. "That was the first time I shook the hand of someone who I consider to be a true American hero," that Ranger said. Leroy Petry "showed that true heroes still exist and that they're closer than you think."

*   *   *

It is impossible to read or hear about such selflessness without wondering, "What compels such courage?" What leads someone like Leroy Peltry to risk everything so that others might live? For answers, we don't need to look far. The roots of Leroy's valor are all around us. They are present in the examples of everyday heroes in our midst who consistently bring out the best in those around them.

Of course, very few of these heroes wear a military uniform. The vast majority are found far from the battlefield.

We see it in parents who make it a priority to instill in their children the importance of honesty, integrity and serving others;

We see it in the compassion of high school teachers who invest extra time to mentor young people who are struggling to keep up, fit in or who just need someone to believe in them;

We see it in the emergency service workers, police officers and all those who risk their lives every day in our cities to keep others safe;

We see it in business people, politicians and pastors who refuse to comprise their values, even when no one would know if they chose otherwise;

And we see it in coaches, counselors and all those every-day heroes whose positive examples inspire us to make going the second mile, second nature.

It is a well-established fact that we look to others for guidance on how to do everything from resolving conflicts, to building our businesses or pursuing our dreams. For example, long before he ever became a Beatle, John Lennon idolized many of the old rhythm and blues greats, people like Chuck Berry and Muddy Waters. He had their pictures on his wall and used them as inspiration when he first began playing the guitar.

In the absence of examples of healthy, empowered, inspiring people, our vision of what is possible in our lives is severely limited. Instead of pushing new bounds and risking moving in different, more empowering directions, we find it easier to play it safe. Allowing our belief in what we can accomplish to be dictated by our experiences rather than liberated by our imaginations.

At the same time, we must never forget that we are always serving as role models to others. In fact, sociologists confirm even the most introverted person in the world will influence at least 10,000 people in their lifetime. No matter who you are, where you work, or what title, position, or rank you possess, you will leave your mark, for good or bad, on scores of people. Helping us all to understand why role modeling is the most powerful message we will ever send to those around us.

How might things change in our world if hero worship didn't disappear with adolescence? What if taking notice of those particularly remarkable people in our lives helped remind us of the value of setting an example worth emulating? So please never forget that heroes aren't limited to famous generals or comic book characters. They're humans like you and me with flaws and frustrations—everyday people who choose to be something more by engaging when others won't and serving when others don't—inspiring everyone around them to consider doing the same.

So my advice to you is simple: choose your heroes and role models wisely, and let them lift you to heights you would not otherwise rise to on your own.

49

Learn to Linger

*"Why hurry over beautiful things? Why
not linger and enjoy them?"*
Clara Schumann

There once was a young man who, with his father, farmed a small piece of land. Several times a year they'd load up the ox cart with vegetables grown in their garden and head off in the direction of the nearest city.

Outside of their name and small family farm, father and son seemed to have little else in common.

The old man believed in pausing to enjoy life's beauty while the son was the go-getter type.

One morning in the summer of 1945, they loaded the cart with produce, hitched their only ox and set out. The young man figured that if they kept a steady pace going all day and night, they could get to the city market by the next morning. He walked alongside the ox and kept prodding it with a stick.

"Take it easy," said his father. "You, and the ox, will last longer."

"If we get to the market ahead of the others," remarked the son, "we have a better chance of getting good prices for our product."

The older man didn't reply. He simply pulled his hat down over his eyes and went to sleep on the seat. Four miles and four hours later, the duo came upon a small house. "Here's your uncle's place," said the father, waking up from his long nap. "Let's stop in and say hello."

"We are already an hour behind schedule," complained the go-getter.

"Then a few more minutes won't matter," replied the father. "My brother and I live so close, yet we see each other so seldom."

The frustrated young man fidgeted while the two older gentleman enjoyed a good cup of tea and shared stories about their families for just over an hour.

On the move again, the father took his turn leading the ox. In just over a mile, they came across a fork in the road. The man directed the ox to go right. "Left is the shorter route," said the son.

"I know," replied the father. "But this way is so much prettier."

"Have you no respect for time?" asked the impatient young man.

"I respect it very much," the father replied. "That's why I like to use it for looking at pretty things. You see, the path to the right leads through the woodlands and passes through a field of magnificent wildflowers."

The young man was unfazed as he was so busy lamenting the time they had lost that he failed to notice the enormous garden of flowers, plants, and lush forest that surrounded them.

"Let's stop and sleep here," remarked the father.

"This is the last trip I will take with you," snapped the son. "You're more interested in gazing at flowers than in making money."

"That's the nicest thing you've said to me in a long time," smiled the older man. A minute later he was sound asleep.

A little before sunrise, the young man shook his father awake. They hitched up the ox and wagon and continued on their journey.

A mile and an hour away they came across upon a farmer trying to pull his cart out of a ditch. "Let's give him a hand," said the father.

"And lose more time?" exploded the son.

"Relax," said the old man. "You might one day find yourself in a ditch."

By the time the boy and the father recommenced their journey, it was almost eight o'clock.

Suddenly a great flash of lightening split the sky. Then there was thunder. Beyond the hills, the heavens grew dark." Looks like a big rain in the city," said the old man.

It wasn't until late afternoon that they got to the top of the hill overlooking the town. They looked down for a long time.

Neither of them spoke.

Finally the young man who had been I such a hurry said, ""I see what you mean, father."

They turned their cart around and headed home from what had once been the city of Hiroshima.

* * *

From the very first time I stumbled across a version of this story in a decades old edition of Readers Digest, I've never forgotten it. The simplicity of the tale and profound message it conveys struck a chord deep within me. Why? Because it reminded me one of the most important lessons a leader can communicate to those around them is the value of *learning to linger.*

According to Webster, to linger is "*to stay somewhere beyond the usual or expected time.*" Lingering. Staying just a bit longer is so hard for me. I'm a type A, get'er done kind of person.

I suspect many of you reading this are, too.

I have long pondered the importance of slowing down, of pausing long enough to reflect on what a particular situation or circumstance could teach me. The problem is, I have not been very successful in actually doing something to periodically interrupt the ever-present pull to hurry along, to get busy pursuing the next thing on my 'to-do' list.

But I decided recently, enough is enough. If I am truly going to live up and into my potential as a leader, at home, at work, in my church, and in my community, I need to spend more time pausing to appreciate, reflect, and learn from life's ordinary moments. To live a more balanced, joy-filled life

How do I begin, you ask? I recommend you start by following the example of the wise man in our story:

> **Take time to rest**...you will be more refreshed, more productive, healthier and happier;

> **Take time to enjoy the company of loved ones**...nothing, and I mean nothing, is more important than nourishing your most important relationships;

> **Take time to enjoy the beauty arrayed around you**...the most incredible man-made work of art cannot get close to the beauty arrayed around you in nature; and,

> **Take time to help someone in need**...as the age-old saying goes, "it is always better to give than to receive."

The bottom line is simple and straightforward: Many of the most precious moments of life occur when we take time to linger.

So today, let me urge you to resist the temptation of falling into the trap of believing that lingering is wasting your time. Let me challenge you to reject the notion that pausing to indulge in a moment of rest, spend extra time with someone you love, savor the splendor of a sunset, or bless someone you encounter in your journey, is anything but time well invested.

I have been learning slowly but surely that there is often no better use of my time than to periodically set aside time to linger.

You should consider giving it a try, yourself.

50

Be a Light to Others

"We are told to let our light shine, and if it does, we won't need to tell anybody it does. Lighthouses don't fire cannons to call attention to their shining–they just shine."
Dwight L. Moody

One of the finest others-centered leaders the world has experienced in the last century is Mother Teresa. This short, frail and unassuming nun chose to make it her life's work to literally care for the common person unable to care for themselves: the sick, the homeless, the outcasts, and the forgotten. Over the course of her life, she worked tirelessly to promote this singular cause. Committed to bringing hope to the hopeless, healing to the hurting, and dignity to the dying, her resolve in being a light in the lives of those experiencing the darkest of moments is perhaps best captured in this brief story of the time she visited Australia.

Shortly after her arrival on the continent, she traveled to a small Aboriginal reservation where she encountered an extremely poor elderly man. As things would have it, this man suffered from mental illness and, as a result, was completely ignored by the people of the small village who did not understand what was wrong with him. As Mother Teresa visited with the destitute man, she quickly saw that the only thing dirtier than his clothing was his tiny home, which apparently had not been cleaned in years.

Overwhelmed with compassion, the elderly nun implored the man to let her clean his house, wash his clothes, and make his bed. He answered, "I'm okay like this. Let it be."

But she persisted, telling him, "You will be better still if you allow me to do this for you."

The man finally agreed, and Mother Teresa went about cleaning his house and washing his clothes. In the midst of her cleaning she discovered a beautiful old lamp, covered with dust. One can only imagine how many years it had been since it had been lit.

She asked the old man, "Don't you light your lamp? Don't you ever use it?"

He quickly answered, "No. No one comes to see me. I have no need to light it. Who would I light it for?"

Mother Teresa quickly responded, "Would you light it every night if one of us would come visit you?"

"Of course," he replied.

From that day forward, sisters from Mother Teresa's order visited the man every day.

They routinely made his bed, cleaned his home, and lit the lamp every evening.

Several years after returning to India, Mother Teresa received a message from the old man that simply said, "Thank you. The light you brought into my life continues to still shine brightly."

*   *   *

Anyone familiar with story of Mother Teresa, a common nun turned modern day saint, recognizes she never chose to shine the spotlight on herself. She had no personal need for recognition. Despite the world taking notice of all she was accomplishing serving the poorest of the poor, as evidenced by her being awarded the 1976 Noble Peace Prize, she always turned any attention she received into an opportunity to promote her cause. She willfully set aside the very human tendency to seek the spotlight, to bask in the glow of being singled out for a job well done. Instead, she humbly chose to make being a light to others the hallmark of her life.

The notion that light is life-giving is nothing new to any of us. In fact, from our earliest days in grade schools we are taught that living organisms are naturally drawn to light, as evidenced by plants naturally leaning toward the window. Science actually has a name for this phenomenon. It's called *the heliotropic effect.*

This effect is defined as the tendency in all living systems to lean into that which gives life and away from that which depletes life—toward positive energy and away from negative energy. Because all living systems have an inclination toward the positive—for example, people remember and learn positive information faster and more accurately than negative information—perhaps it should be no surprise that human brains are activated more by positivity than by negativity. As Kim Cameron of the University of Michigan reminds us, "Leaders that capitalize on the positive, similarly tend to produce life-giving, flourishing outcomes in organizations. A focus on the positive is life-giving for individuals and organizations in the same way that positive energy in nature enhances thriving in living organisms."

In a world prone to ascribe value to someone based more on how they look, who they know, what they drive or where they live, people are hungry for leaders willing to transcend superficiality and celebrate originality. We yearn for leaders willing to judge less and serve more, just as we are desperate for leaders who understand that, in leadership, shining the light of positivity can do more to elevate performance, enhance engagement and contribute to creating a healthy culture than virtually anything else. What can you do to be a light to others today? Consider asking yourself:

- Am I doing all I can to express gratitude and appreciation each day to those around me?

- How often and how consistently am I encouraging or recognizing others for a job well done?
- Is there something I can be doing in my personal sphere of influence to more effectively build an environment where blunders and mistakes are forgiven and grudges are not held?
- How can I inspire others to be more otherly with those around them?

As the inspiring and enduring example of noble laureate Mother Teresa reminds us, the most successful leaders in history choose not to absorb the light but, rather, reflect it. They demonstrate through their actions that true satisfaction stems from willfully deflecting the desire to accumulate accolades for ourselves and, instead, humbly embrace opportunities to fulfill the legitimate needs of those around us. For in choosing to be a source of positive energy wherever we may be called to serve, we enable those around us to tap into a special reservoir of strength—a reservoir that equips, encourages, empowers and ideally inspires others to become all they are capable of becoming.

Remember, you don't have to be a saint to add tangible value in the world. All you need to do is be on the lookout for opportunities to be a light in someone's life, so they too can burn bright enough for the entire world to see.

Why not get started immediately?

51

Seek the Coin of the Realm

"Waste no more time arguing what a good man should be. Be one."
Marcus Aurelius

There is a famous story of a nobleman, Sir Philip Sidney, who, fighting for his beloved England in the sixteenth century, was mortally wounded on the battlefield. Though he was desperately thirsty from loss of blood, he chose to do the unexpected and gave away his water flask to a dying young soldier. His final words, "Thy necessity is yet greater than mine," serve as a stark contrast to how the majority of people of power, privilege, and position of his era would have likely acted in that moment, had they found themselves facing the same choice.

Examples of leaders like Sir Philip Sydney provide us with living, breathing definitions of *character*. And although we use this word frequently, we rarely take the time to fully unpack and understand it, despite its almost unquantifiable significance to us as human beings.

The word *character* derives from a Greek word that means 'to mark', which originates from the centuries-old practice of engraving the likeness of important figures on metal coins. Be it emperors, kings, or heroes, the appearance of a distinctive, difficult-to-forge caricature on silver or some other form of precious metal was designed to build trust and facilitate mutually beneficial transactions between people.

Character continues to do the same for us today.

In simplest terms, your character is how you choose to walk in the world. It's the inward values that determine outward actions. It's what defines you as a person, both inside and out. Although there is no consensus on a definition of character or agreement on the best way to develop character, I find the following description written years ago by an anonymous author summarizes it best: "Everything begins in our mind as a thought. Our thoughts become our words. What we choose to think and say influence our actions. Our actions become our habits. Our habits constitute our character and our character is what ultimately shapes our legacy. Character, then, is the sum of the choices we make in life, for better or worse."

Study after study continues to validate the premium we place on character. In research involving twenty-five thousand leaders rated by more than two hundred thousand evaluators, character was identified as the quintessential quality that distinguishes great performers from the rest of the pack. Similarly, an independent study conducted by the Corporate Leadership Council found that team members identified character as the most desirable attribute for both coworkers and supervisors alike.

As important as character is for us we must recognize becoming and staying a leader with character is not a static phenomenon. Character evolves and grows stronger (for better or worse) on an ongoing basis. You cannot expect to read a leadership book, go to a training seminar or sit through a Sunday sermon and suddenly be transformed into a leader with character. Becoming someone others believe in, want to follow and, ideally, want to emulate, is a lifelong pursuit. It's a process of ongoing personal development and daily refinement that leads you to make excellence the hallmark of your life.

So what can you do to intentionally invest in your character development? Consider starting with these three areas:

Evaluate your life. Are you living by your guidelines? An important step in strengthening your character is taking an inventory of your past behaviors/choices and, more importantly, your current behaviors and choices. Are you thinking and acting in line with your values—your deeply held beliefs that describe the person you strive to be? If you answer yes, then commit to staying the course. But if you answer no, then you need to ask yourself some hard questions about why you're making the choices you are and determine what you can begin doing differently to get yourself back on track.

Do your actions match your intentions? Sociologists tell us that even the most introverted person in the world will influence at least 10,000 people in their lifetime. No matter who you are, where you work, or what title, position, rank, or role you possess, you will leave your mark, for good or bad, on scores of people. It's easy to lose sight of the significant impact you have on others and, as a result, you may forget to pause from time-to-time to assess if your 'talk' is consistently matching your 'walk'. Do your actions and intentions align? If not, why not?

Decide what needs to change in your own life ... and then move out! After acknowledging where you may be making choices that lead you to act inconsistently with the person you strive to be, commit to doing something about it. For example, do you desire to be more honest with others? Are you ready to let go of manipulating others to get what you want from them? Whatever changes you plan to make, write them down. Ponder them. Then resolve to do something about them ... one choice at a time.

Character is not a light switch of sorts that we simply turn on or off. It takes work to become the person we want to be and others deserve to see. Fortunately, every day we encounter situations that present a different experience to learn and deepen character. The question is, what will you choose to do with these opportunities?

52

Remain True to Your Word

"Men acquire a particular quality by
constantly acting in a particular way."
Aristotle

Few leaders it seems, especially those serving in politics, are able to
live up to the lofty ideal of being considered a stalwart of character
and integrity. However, Abraham Lincoln most certainly qualifies as
one such man.

Most people are aware of Lincoln's numerous failures before he
became president, as the stories are widely circulated: failed romantic
relationships, failed business ventures, and failed political campaigns.
The list of failures was long indeed. But one failure that has never
been attributed to this great man is a failure to live up to his legendary
commitment to honesty.

In fact, stories abound of how Lincoln never forgot the lessons born
of his failures and hardships, choosing instead to let these lessons forge
his character and solidify his commitment to doing the right things
for the right reasons. One example of this is the time Lincoln found
out that an old woman in dire poverty, the widow of a Revolutionary
soldier, had been charged a $200 fee for getting her husband's $400
pension. Lincoln, outraged at this injustice, sued the pension agent and
won the case for the old woman. In fact, he didn't even charge her for

his services; instead, he gave her money for a ticket home and paid her hotel bill in full during the hearing.

Some may also be familiar with the story of the time Lincoln was hired to work for a business owner named Denton Offutt, who owned a general store in New Salem, Illinois. Following one of his afternoon shifts, Lincoln noticed that a man overpaid him and had left before Lincoln found the mistake. So, before returning home for the night, Lincoln chose to walk several miles out of his way to give the man back his change—four cents!

Though this story of Abraham Lincoln, the honest shop clerk, is fairly well known, the less familiar story of Abraham Lincoln as the honest shop owner is not. Yet it reveals the depth of his commitment to being a leader who could be counted on to always be upright in principle and action.

While still living in New Salem, Lincoln and a partner bought a general store and attempted to run it as a profitable business. But owing to unwise investments and poor management, the store eventually went bankrupt. Shortly thereafter, his partner in the store died, leaving Lincoln saddled with enormous debt from the failed venture. Unlike many others who experienced failed businesses and chose instead to skip town to escape their creditors, Lincoln promised to repay every cent he owed, which was something he indeed accomplished, although it took him more than 15 years to do so.

As the story reveals, when Abraham Lincoln made a commitment, it was clear he was true to his word. No circumstance or individual could keep him from living a life of complete honesty and genuine transparency. His was a life marked by consistent displays of integrity, truth, and sincerity—a life void of the fraud, deceit, and mistrust that make it impossible to grow into a respected leader.

Now, I know that Abraham Lincoln is the high watermark of positive leadership. His rare blend of tenacity, humility, and wisdom certainly marks him as an iconic leader for the ages. That said, Abe Lincoln-like honesty is certainly one attribute we can all choose to emulate in our own spheres of influence. If you agree, here are three simple considerations from Lincoln's own words to help get you started:

Always be truthful: *"Once you forfeit the confidence of your fellow-citizens, you can never regain their respect and esteem."*

Honesty is the key to trust, and trust is required to improve your relationship with others. Although it's not much in fashion these days to talk about the benefits of honesty and decency, the benefits are there nonetheless and warrant discussion. Honesty, as we've seen in the example of great leaders like Abraham Lincoln, is characterized by truth and sincerity. It's consistently demonstrating in word and deed that you are someone who values integrity over popularity, who prefers candor to slander and chooses to promote selflessness rather than selfishness.

Be true to you: *"I am not bound to win, but I am bound to be true. I am not bound to succeed, but I am bound to live by the light that I have."*

In simplest terms, honesty helps reveal the true nature of your character. After all, if you can't be trusted in a small matter, how can you be trusted to be honest in bigger things? Hence, being honest means being true first and foremost to yourself. It's about being real—and accepting--of yourself, warts and all. If you don't pretend to be someone you're not, then people already know what they can expect from you, and you can spend more time focused on achieving your goals and no time worrying about building or sustaining a facade.

Expect the best by resolving to be and do your best: *"I do the very best I know how – the very best I can; and I mean to keep on doing so until the end."*

Ambition can either be the fuel that propels you to your goals or persuades you to cut corners. Fight the urge to achieve success at any cost. Set the bar high, but don't become so enamored with the prize that you risk what matters most—your reputation. Don't lower your expectations to meet your performance. Raise your level of performance to meet your expectations. Insist on expecting the best of yourself, and then do what is necessary to legitimately make it a reality.

As these three simple lessons from Honest Abe remind us, honesty seeds trust in our homes, workplaces, worship spaces, and communities and, most importantly, is the keystone of our credibility as leaders. Being trustworthy demonstrates you understand that character cannot be developed merely in ease and quiet. But rather, only through the occasional experience of trial and suffering can the soul be strengthened, ambition inspired, and success achieved.

Resolve today to always remain true to you. Let your example be a source of inspiration to those around you.

Unlocking Victory: The Final Soundbite

"I find the great thing in this world is not so much
where we stand, as in what direction we are moving:
To reach the port of heaven, we must sail sometimes
with the wind and sometimes against it, but we
must sail, and not drift, nor lie at anchor."
Oliver Wendell Holmes, Jr.

As I mentioned at the outset of our journey together, human beings are moved by stories. Stories stir the soul, ignite the imagination and engage our hearts and minds in ways no other medium can. And this is my final input to this story.

The mission we had in Afghanistan was unique in that every day, we were expected to interact with our Afghan partners for one primary reason – to help them create a better story. We served alongside men and women who hope for a better, brighter future for themselves, their families and their country. Every day they looked to each of us to set an example worth emulating.

What a privilege.

What a great story.

Our unlikely story of building an independent, capable, and sustainable Air Force in an active war zone was that of a team of people working diligently far from the limelight in support of a noble cause; a team of people trying to do their small part to help move a nation beyond its current challenges, so that its citizens could enjoy a life of greater meaning, purpose and abundance. It's a story about the power of dedicated professionals striving to transform good people into great leaders in their own right. It's a story about what is possible when individuals give their all to try and leave their part of the world a little better than they first found it.

History reminds us that the reason all world-changers and universe benders lived great stories is because they, and those around them, knew exactly what they wanted. Be it racial equality, liberation from oppression, dignity for the poor, or the establishment of a more just society – those throughout time who succeeded in adding tangible value to their surroundings understood promoting positive progress isn't easy...but then again, nothing worth doing ever is.

As I wrap up *The Art of Positive Leadership*, I would like to leave you with one final story.

An ancient legend tells of a general whose army was afraid to fight. Though they doubted their potential, he did not. Though they were unsure of their abilities, he was not. He knew they were strong and capable. He knew without question his team could win.

Pondering how he could infuse them with the confidence and conviction needed to take new ground, the general had an idea. He assembled his soldiers and told them he possessed a magical coin–a prophetic coin–a coin which would always accurately foretell the outcome of the battle. On one side was the image of an eagle. The eagle represented courage, perseverance, strength and leadership. The other side of the coin bore the image of a serpent. It represented cunning, deception, and surprise. He would toss the coin. If it landed eagle-side up, they would win. If it landed serpent-side up, they would lose.

The army was silent as the coin flipped end-over-end in the air. Soldiers encircled the general so they could see the coin hit the ground.

They held their breath and then shouted when they saw the eagle. Infused with a renewed sense of possibility, the army believed they would win.

Bolstered by their new-found assurance of victory, the soldiers marched forward against the enemy stronghold and won...confidently; courageously; decisively.

It was only after the victory that the king showed his soldiers the coin. The two sides were identical. The symbol of the mighty eagle was engraved on both front and back.

Though the story is fictional, the truth is reliable. Confidence, courage and decisiveness are the keys that unlock victory.

*   *   *

To be clear, it was difficult enough to build an Air Force in peacetime, but training and developing sophisticated capabilities and integrating new technologies while concurrently fighting and winning a war was unprecedented. All of this was happening, mind you, with limited time, diminishing financial resources, fewer people and scores of logistics and supply challenges. Add in a culture that is hungry for positive change but lacks so many of the elements many of us take for granted in western society, and it was easy to believe we had been asked to pull off mission impossible.

Yet, nothing could be further from the reality of what actually occurred.

You see, despite widespread illiteracy, a resilient and determined enemy, a largely tribe-centered culture, seemingly forever competing political factions and a score of other factors reflective of a culture at war for over three decades, progress abounded. Why? One reason— confident, courageous and decisive *others-centered* leadership.

Never in my adult life had I been surrounded by so many inspiring men and women committed to doing their part to write a better story for a nation hungry for hope and change. At no time in my career can I remember having the great privilege of working alongside so many accomplished professionals who, despite the daunting nature of their circumstances, chose to selflessly give their best to serve their fellow man. Be it American, Croatian, Greek, Czech, Mongol, Turk, Hungarian, Italian, or any of the fourteen nations who were part of this one-of-a-kind command, each and every person was courageously committed to equipping, encouraging, empowering, and inspiring, those around them.

And the results speak for themselves.

The selfless actions of the warrior-leaders of NATO Air Training Command–Afghanistan contributed to unprecedented positive progress. Airpower capacity grew by over 200 percent; scores of lives were saved, battles were won; billions of dollars were saved and, just as importantly, a renewed sense of potential was restored. As a result of the team's efforts, Afghanistan is now stronger and more capable. Confidence, conviction, perseverance, strength and leadership was infused in the members of the Afghan Air Force and a renewed sense of possibility has been awakened. Because of the consistent application and reinforcement of the principles described in *The Art of Positive Leadership*, our Afghan partners are marching steadily forward... confidently, courageously; decisively.

As I reach the close of our time together, I would like to leave you with one of my favorite quotes from the late, great Ralph Waldo Emerson. I love these words because they paint a vivid picture of what true success—in life and in leadership—is all about:

> "To laugh often and much; To win the respect of intelligent people and the affection of children; To earn the appreciation of honest critics and endure the betrayal of false friends; To appreciate beauty, to find the best in others; To leave the world a bit better, whether by a healthy child, a garden patch or a redeemed social condition; To know even one life has breathed easier because you have lived. *This is to have succeeded.*"

The need to reimagine and recast how we think about leadership has never been greater. In my view, too many of us have allowed our understanding of leadership to grow stagnant, contributing to why we face so many daunting problems in our society today. As so many workplaces continue to struggle with record low engagement and productivity levels, it is clear people want a more expressive, intuitive, and authentic style of leader. People everywhere are eager to encounter an *others-centered* leader who routinely demonstrates kindness and empathy, uses influence rather than control to exercise their power, and is unafraid to equip, encourage, empower, and inspire others in their own leadership journey.

I am forever grateful for the opportunity to have been part of a team intent on exercising the confidence, courage and decisiveness to make the mission of building an independent, sustainable and capable Afghan Air Force an emerging reality. I am humbled to have contributed to creating conditions for a safer, stronger, more resilient Afghanistan to emerge. And I appreciate you, the reader, have afforded me the privilege of sharing this story.

CONTINUE THE MISSION

Ready to continue the mission? Please go to **www.JohnEMichel.com** and share your stories of those leaders in your midst who exemplify the principles outlined in this book.

ABOUT THE AUTHOR

John is a TEDx speaker, author, business advisor, and widely-recognized expert in culture, social media, strategy & individual and organizational change. A recently retired Air Force General, he is also the founder and senior curator of the world's largest senior military leader blog platform at *GeneralLeadership.com*. An accomplished, unconventional leader and proven status quo buster, John is the only senior military leader to successfully design and lead several international, multi-billion dollar transformation efforts. His award-winning work has been featured in a wide variety of articles and journals, including the *Harvard Business Review*, *Fast Company*, *Huffington Post*, *National Geographic*, *Joint Forces Quarterly*, and the *Washington Post*. You can learn more about John at his website, *www.JohnEMichel.com*, or reach out to him on Twitter at *@JohnEMichel*.